CONSTRUCTION
TENDERING
and
ESTIMATING

CONSTRUCTION TENDERING and ESTIMATING

J.I.W. Bentley ARICS, MCIOB

London
E. & F.N. SPON

First published in 1987 by E. & F.N. Spon Ltd.
11 New Fetter Lane, London EC4P 4EE

© 1987   J.I.W. Bentley

Printed in Great Britain at the University Press,
Cambridge

ISBN 0 419 14240 1

British Library Cataloguing in Publication Data

Bentley, J.I.W.
  Construction tendering and estimating.
  1. Building—Estimates
  I. Title
  624   TH435

ISBN 0-419-14240-1

CONTENTS

PREFACE

To obtain work, building contractors must submit tenders of one form or another, and for this to happen, estimates of the probable cost must be prepared. It follows that these estimates must be as accurate as possible in order that the contractor may not only obtain work, but obtain that work at such a price as to make a profit and stay in business.

An essential first step is to have a clear, logical approach to the preparation of an estimate, and it is hoped that this book will assist the reader to achieve this laudable aim. It will be appreciated however that an estimator, besides following the procedure advocated here, must have a comprehensive knowledge of the technical processes of construction. The estimator also requires adequate feedback and support from the rest of the building team.

This book attempts to act as a foundation course for students either aspiring to become estimators, or requiring a basic knowledge of estimating techniques and tendering procedures. In particular, due regard has been taken of the B/TEC syllabus 'Tendering and Estimating' at level IV. Students studying for the examinations of the Chartered Institute of Building, Royal Institution of Chartered Surveyors, and degrees in Building and Quantity Surveying should also find that this book provides for their essential requirements.

Civil engineering students should also find that they will be able to adapt the principles advocated here to their particular needs in estimating, which, although perhaps on a larger scale for individual operations of work, nevertheless require the same general approach as for building work. Certainly the author found this to be the case in his own experience of tendering for dams and bridges.

Each chapter may be read in isolation, which should prove useful for someone with a basic knowledge of the subject, and also for the student who may wish to refer to a specific aspect.

Reference is frequently made to a hypothetical project, the construction of a three-storey office block, so that the reader, it is hoped, may follow more clearly the activities to be performed in preparing a tender from the initial decision to tender, to the submission of the tender.

The Code of Estimating Practice, published by the Chartered Institute of Building, acts as a comprehensive guide to the various activities to be performed in estimating, and would be a useful additional reference especially for an assistant estimator.

Spon's Architects' and Builders' Price Book, published annually, is also an invaluable reference. I have often used this book as: a guide to prices generally; a source of rates for minor but frequent items, thus saving much time; and for approximate estimating on an elemental basis. Since there are over 20 000 prices, each with labour time details, Spon's may be somewhat intimidating to students. However a little patience and application will work wonders enabling a grasp of relative values to be obtained. Used with this text, it should be of great help in project work.

Emphasis in this book is laid on principles. We live in an age of change, and therefore the very latest information should be consulted regarding relevant legislation, working rules, wage agreements, and so on. It is suggested that a valuable exercise would be to up-date the calculations in the text, and for this purpose blank columns are provided in price tables so that current prices can be inserted by the reader. Students are also encouraged to answer the self-assessment questions appended to the chapters.

ACKNOWLEDGMENTS

I wish to acknowledge with thanks the help given to me by: the late Trevor Morton of Leeds College of Building; W.P.L. Stewart of John Laing Construction; C.T. Emsley of N.G. Bailey and Co. Ltd., Ian Bancroft of the Marshall Construction Group; and my former colleagues at the School of Constructional Studies, Leeds Polytechnic in either checking the text or giving helpful suggestions. The Value of Output Table—Housing and Construction Statistics is reproduced by kind permission of the Controller of Her Majesty's Stationery Office.

JIWB
1987

1

TENDERING

CHAPTER OBJECTIVES

After studying this chapter you should be able to:

- appreciate the main types and sources of building work;

- understand the appropriate methods of tendering and the relevant tender documents.

1.1 THE MARKET

1.1.1 External influences affecting the construction industry market

Central government, directly and indirectly, has a great influence on the amount of work that is available within the construction industry. In recent years public sector spending on the construction of schools, housing, public buildings and roads has been cut back, but could equally well be increased by an upturn in the economy and/or a change in government policy.

Interest rates—whether rising or falling—affect the cost of all building work to a greater or lesser degree, and will consequently influence a decision on whether or not to build. The availability of mortgages and loans of all kinds will also have a profound influence on the state of the building market.

Rises in world oil prices and other fuel costs have meant that a great emphasis is now laid on energy savings, requiring such measures as increased insulation for buildings of all kinds. Specialized markets have thus been created, for example, in wall and ceiling insulation and double glazing.

Table 1.1 Value of output[1]

£million

| | New housing | | Other new work | | | All new work | Repair and maintenance | | | All repair and mainten-ance | All work |
| | Public | Private | Public | Private | | | Housing | Other work | | | |
				Industrial	Commercial			Public	Private		
(a) At current prices											
1983	1 120	3 729	3 729	1 850	2 967	13 396	5 622	3 548	1 777	10 948	24 343
1984	1 077	3 831	3 833	2 342	3 110	14 192	6 251	3 746	2 014	12 011	26 203
1985	918	3 848	3 786	2 848	3 520	14 921	6 809	3 800	2 321	12 930	27 850
1984 1	279	943	894	459	721	3 296	1 487	896	450	2 832	6 128
2	266	962	973	562	782	3 545	1 583	892	481	2 955	6 500
3	275	972	1 043	664	820	3 772	1 650	993	534	3 177	6 949
4	257	954	923	658	787	3 579	1 531	966	550	3 047	6 626
1985 1	224	917	870	645	763	3 419	1 629	972	538	3 139	6 558
2	237	921	964	746	881	3 750	1 642	890	569	3 101	6 851
3	241	978	1 007	744	957	3 927	1 801	936	584	3 320	7 248
4	216	1 032	945	712	920	3 824	1 737	1 003	630	3 370	7 194
1986 1P	194	996	878	623	904	3 594	1 672	922	587	3 180	6 774
(b) At 1980 prices seasonally adjusted											
1983	1 001	3 238	3 556	1 879	3 014	12 688	4 326	2 711	1 377	8 413	21 101
1984	910	3 118	3 599	2 354	3 147	13 128	4 532	2 694	1 468	8 693	21 821
1985	751	2 968	3 396	2 702	3 375	13 182	4 688	2 595	1 607	8 889	22 072

1984	1	243	837	917	511	769	3 277	1 102	657	352	2 111	5 388
	2	229	764	923	582	812	3 309	1 162	649	355	2 167	5 476
	3	224	762	895	616	791	3 288	1 183	711	356	2 249	5 538
	4	215	754	864	645	775	3 253	1 084	677	404	2 166	5 419
1985	1	188	763	859	687	790	3 286	1 144	675	397	2 215	5 502
	2	196	708	868	719	859	3 350	1 146	615	400	2 161	5 511
	3	190	736	825	643	860	3 255	1 223	635	375	2 233	5 488
	4	177	760	844	654	856	3 291	1 175	670	435	2 280	5 571
1986	1P	159	764	833	621	875	3 251	1 124	613	416	2 153	5 405

(c) Indices at 1980 prices seasonally adjusted

1980 = 100

1983		58.5	125.2	100.9	67.0	124.1	97.2	96.5	92.9	86.2	93.5	95.7
1984		53.2	120.6	102.1	83.9	129.5	100.6	101.1	92.3	91.9	96.6	99.0
1985		43.9	114.8	96.4	96.3	138.5	101.0	104.6	88.9	100.6	98.8	100.1
1984	1	56.7	129.5	104.1	72.9	126.6	100.4	98.4	90.0	88.3	93.9	97.7
	2	53.5	118.3	104.8	82.9	133.7	101.4	103.8	88.9	89.0	96.3	99.3
	3	52.3	118.0	101.6	87.8	130.2	100.8	105.6	97.4	89.1	100.0	100.5
	4	50.3	116.7	98.1	92.0	127.6	99.7	96.8	92.7	101.3	96.3	98.3
1985	1	43.9	118.1	97.5	97.9	130.0	100.7	102.1	92.5	99.4	98.5	99.8
	2	45.9	109.5	98.5	102.5	141.5	102.7	102.3	84.3	100.3	96.1	100.0
	3	44.4	114.0	93.7	91.7	141.6	99.7	109.2	87.0	93.9	99.3	99.5
	4	41.4	117.7	95.8	93.2	140.8	100.8	104.9	91.8	108.9	101.4	101.0
1986	1P	37.2	118.2	94.5	88.5	144.0	99.6	100.4	84.0	104.1	95.7	98.0

1 Output by contractors, including estimates of unrecorded output by small firms and self-employed workers and output by public sector direct labour departments, classified to construction in the 1980 Standard Industrial Classification.
P Projected figures.
(Source: *Housing and Construction Statistics*)

1.1.2 Types of work

The type of work available to the building industry ranges from minor repair work costing only a few pounds to major projects that cost many millions. Large building contracts call for many of the methods and machines that we associate with the civil engineering industry. Table 1.1 gives an indication of the relative importance from 1983 to 1986 of the various categories of work in both the building and Civil Engineering industries.

Scope of Table 1.1

The value of output figures include the following categories of work:

- erecting and repairing buildings of all types;
- constructing and repairing roads and bridges;
- erecting steel and reinforced concrete structures;
- other civil engineering work, such as laying sewers;
- overhead lines, extracting coal from open cast workings, etc.

Housing and Construction Statistics are prepared and published quarterly by the Department of the Environment. A 'notes and definitions' supplement is published annually.

Changes in the relative importance of work

Besides giving the actual values of the various categories of work, Table 1.1 also shows the changes in their relative importance which occur over a number of years. For example Table 1.2 summarizes figures from Table 1.1(a).

These figures show an increase in the relative expenditure on private housing between 1983 and 1985 – but they are quoted at current prices.

Table 1.2 Relative expenditure on public and private housing, 1983/85

Year	New housing		£ million
	Public	Private	Total
1983	1120	3729	4849
1985	918	3848	4766

Expressed as relative percentage this gives:

Year	Public	Private
1983	23	77
1985	19	81

If we wish to compare the actual value of work in real terms from year to year, the figures have to be adjusted to take account of the effect of inflation. This has been done in Table 1.1(b), which gives the value of output at 1980 prices seasonally adjusted. This has been expressed in relative terms in Table 1.1(c), which shows indices at 1980 prices seasonally adjusted.

Overseas work

Construction work worth many millions of pounds is carried out overseas in building and civil engineering projects. This overseas work provides employment for supervisory staff and skilled workers from Britain, and in many cases produces contracts for materials and equipment to be supplied by British companies.

The risks encountered overseas with respect to costs and payments are usually many times greater than those faced at home. Thus even greater attention must be paid to market opportunities and contractual obligations when tendering for overseas work.

Builder-generated work

Speculative housing forms the largest part of the private new housing market in Britain. In this area the example that comes readily to mind is that of 'Barratts' who in 1981 built some 11 000 dwellings on land they had purchased previously. They, like many other companies, were acting therefore as both developer and builder. Alternatively, a developer may initiate a scheme by obtaining or providing the necessary capital, buying the land, and employing consultants to design the dwellings, and then contract with a builder to erect them.

A potential demand may also be converted into sales by a builder advertising, for example, a package of design and build for kitchens or other extensions.

Many such extensions, or even complete houses, are now prefabricated, and are often promoted by large companies who can, by their name and reputation, assure clients that they can be confident of the quality and guarantees that are offered.

1.1.3 Marketing

A building company may set about generating business in a number of ways. But for any marketing strategy to be successful two important requirements must be met: accurate information must be gathered about the current and future state of the market; and the company must promote its image among potential clients.

Marketing opportunities through planning registers

All planning authorities are required to keep a register of planning applications received and the outcome of such applications. This forms the basis of a valuable information source, covering all forms of new and often refurbishment work for the marketing oriented builder.

Anyone has the right to inspect these registers, and since most proposed work requires planning approval, frequent visits to the local planning office can generate a considerable number of potential clients.

Source of up-to-date information

Since marketing is related to time the most up-to-date information is required. Although historical records of output are of interest in indicating trends, it is the work at the design stage and coming out to tender that is usually of most use, since builders are concerned with the future workload. Information may be obtained from such publications as: *Building, The Contracts Journal, The Building Trades Journal, The Financial Times* and statistics prepared by the Department of the Environment. Additionally there are specialist firms who offer regular reports on planning applications and approvals to subscribers.

Sales promotion

This has been touched on above, but is sadly neglected by most builders. A vigorous policy of promoting a company's image needs to be pursued to gain the confidence of clients and promote sales. All areas of contact, with both present and possible future clients, need to be examined so that the best possible image can be presented.

1.2 THE CLIENT

The most important person is of course the provider of work—the client. Clients can be divided into two broad divisions: private and public clients. Private clients vary from a householder who requires a small repair or alteration costing only a few pounds, to the large multi-national corporation that requires a multi-million pound industrial complex to be constructed to exacting standards within a fixed budget and time. Similarly public bodies—be they small local authorities or the Property Services Agency that acts for central government—will vary in their requirements. Local authorities and central government agencies spend public money, and consequently must place contracts in such a manner that the best value for money is seen to be obtained. Thus a small private client may employ a builder directly with the assistance of an architect and/or other consultants as necessary, whereas a public authority has to employ a formal procedure so that it may readily be seen to obtain a competitive price fairly and equitably. Large companies (corporate clients) have to operate in a similar manner to public authorities since their directors are answerable to shareholders.

1.3 CONTRACTUAL ARRANGEMENTS

Since such a variety of work and wide diversity of clients exist, it is not surprising that a choice of contractual arrangements is available that is designed to provide the most satisfactory solution to suit particular circumstances.

1.3.1 Types of contract

The three main groups into which building contracts can be divided are as follows:

- *Lump Sum Contracts*. The price to be paid is agreed in advance, but is subject to increases or decreases as a result of any necessary adjustment for variations, prime cost and provisional sums or price fluctuations.
- *Measurement Contracts*. The price to be paid is obtained by measurement and valuation as work proceeds and is related to a contract schedule of prices.
- *Cost Reimbursement Contracts*. Payment is on the basis of the actual cost incurred by the contractor in carrying out the work, plus an agreed amount to allow for overheads and profit.

There are many permutations of the above types of contractual arrangements depending on such considerations as the technical expertise available, both in the consultant's and the contractor's area, and the market conditions. Thus we get contracts based upon bills of quantities, or drawings and specifications, and contracts being negotiated perhaps on the basis of two-stage tendering. The most appropriate contractual arrangements in the client's interest should be adopted, and the commonest are now described.

Selective tendering

Selective tendering was recommended in the Banwell Report of 1964 (The Placing and Management of Building and Civil Engineering Contracts) and is now the method generally adopted. This is because the cost of preparing a tender is considerable and the successful tender has to bear the cost of all the unsuccessful tenders prepared by that particular firm. Further it will be recognised that the tender figure, which forms the basis of the contract sum, may be very different from the final account figure and thus the final cost to the client. Contractors are invited to tender on their reputation, thus their past performance as regards capability, quality and completion on time is taken into account.

1.3.2 Continuity contracts

Many cases arise where a series of contracts, or an extension of the scope and extent of an existing contract, is required and three such cases are now considered.

(a) *Serial contracts*

Where a definite programme of related work can be envisaged, such as a number of schools or a building to be constructed in several phases over a period of time, then continuity in the use of resources can be achieved by employing one contractor. The work should then be carried out more economically than if it were handled by several different contractors. The first contract is usually let on a competitive tender, and the preamble states that further work may be negotiated using the priced bill of quantities as a basis. This further work is usually described giving an indication of its scope and timing. When the additional work is designed, the tender documents are prepared and the contract is negotiated and signed; thus control is exercised over each phase of work whatever the size.

(b) *Continuation contracts*

This is more of an *ad hoc* arrangement since at the time of tendering for the original contract further work may not be envisaged as more than a possibility. The case may arise that during the construction of say a factory a combination of circumstances, such as increased demand for the manufactured products and availability of adjacent land with planning permission, means that another factory unit is required to be started as soon as possible. Thus, perhaps before the first factory has been completed, a second one may be started. The contractor is usually willing to negotiate the second contract in a similar manner to a serial contract, and again economics of scale and continuity may be achieved.

(c) *Term contracts*

These contracts are mostly used where extensive repair and maintenance work is required over a fixed period of time or, 'term'. Since the extent of such work is difficult to envisage, the tendering document is usually a schedule of rates—a measurement contract. The Property Services Agency's schedule of rates is the most comprehensive document of its kind. Term contracts may be made with specialist sub-contractors as well as with general builders, the orders and supervision being carried out by the client's technical staff, such as building surveyors or maintenance supervisors.

(d) *Feedback*

On serial, and to a lesser extent on continuation contracts, feedback can be provided from the contractor to the architects and consulting engineers to make for more efficient construction. This feedback can range from advice on the practicality of the methods of construction, to specific design details such as damp proofing.

1.3.3 Design-and-build contracts

Design-and-build contracts (often known as package-deal contracts) involve the highest degree of contractor involvement, and thus the feedback from construction problems met on site enables the best possible use to be made of the contractor's knowledge of construction and organization. The client is usually best advised to employ a chartered quantity surveyor, independent of the contractor, whose sole purpose is to look after the client's interests and to ensure 'value for money spent'! Initially several contractors may be asked to submit a draft design and budget based upon performance criteria for a particular site. The client's quantity surveyor, or other consultants, plays a most important role at this time in assessing not only the practicality of each scheme but the best solutions in respect of the client's design and economic criteria. Detailed designs are then finalized and the price negotiated.

The design may be carried out by the contractor's own design staff or outside architects may be commissioned by the contractor.

The most suitable projects for this type of contract seem to be those where speed is important—from inception to completion—and where there are advantages to be gained from the contractor using his expertise to advise the design team on specialized types of construction.

1.3.4 Management contracts

Management contracts are another relatively new form of contracting, designed to achieve completion of a project to the required performance standards of quality and time, by achieving a closer association between the professions and the contractor. The management contractor manages all the resources employed on the project and, usually, does not execute any work directly, except for the provision of those items of cost usually specified in the preliminaries, such as welfare facilities, temporary services and general hoisting facilities. To be most effective the management contractor should be brought in at the design stage to give programming, construction and costing advice and assistance.

A budget, or estimated prime cost, should be established initially to enable financial control to be exercised over the project. Such a budget is essential in order that the client may meet construction costs when they become due and to plan fiscally for the final outcome.

1.4 TENDER DOCUMENTS

The tender documents will depend on the contractual arrangements, and in the most common situation, i.e. a lump sum contract based upon bills of quantities, will consist of the following:

- Bills of quantities—including particulars of the conditions of contract.
- Location drawings—these being selected from the contract drawings with a list being given in the preambles of the drawings from which the bills of quantities have been prepared and which will be available for inspection.
- Two copies of the form of tender.

Where the lump sum is required for works of a minor nature, or for civil engineering contracts that may be quite large, then bills of quantities may be dispensed with and the tender documents will consist of:

- The specification, including particulars of the conditions of contract.
- Drawings identical to the contract drawings to define the full extent of the work.
- Two copies of the form of tender.

In this case the contractor has to prepare a bill of quantities sufficient for the preparation of his tender.

It should be noted that in the first case where the bills of quantities are a tender document and eventually a contract document, any errors have to be corrected and the contract sum amended. Individual rates and percentages entered by the contractor also play a significant part in the valuation of the works in progress and the agreement of the final account.

In the second case where the bills of quantities are prepared for the contractor's own use, any errors are not corrected and do not alter the contract sum. Further, the valuations and final account calculations may be more difficult particularly if there are significant variations. This problem may be only partly solved by the provision of a schedule of rates, or by lump sums being inserted against items in the specification.

1.5 THE CLIENT'S ADMINISTRATIVE PROCEDURE

This section might be called, 'How tenders are obtained by the client and the contract awarded.' Single-stage selective tendering is the most usual and suitable method of obtaining competitive tenders for the majority of building works.

1.5.1 Single-stage selective tendering

The Code of Procedure for Single Stage Selective Tendering 1977 prepared by the National Joint Consultative Committee for Building and approved by the Department of the Environment sets out a recommended procedure and four of the most important recommendations are now described.

(a) The number of tenders should be restricted and the following is given as a guide:

Size of contract	Maximum number of tenders
Up to £50 000	5
£50 000 to £250 000	6
£250 000 to £1 million	8
£1 million+	6

(b) The contract period should be given so that there is only one variable—the tender sum.
(c) The time allowed for tendering should be fixed in relation to the size and complexity of the job. A minimum of four weeks should be allowed, but major works and smaller works based on drawings and specifications, without quantities, may require a longer period. Any tenders that are received late should be returned unopened and not considered.
(d) Notification of results should be made as soon as the contract has been let. A list of the firms in alphabetical order and the tender figures in ascending order should be given. This assists contractors in forming an intelligent view of their future tendering strategy and thus enables them to make their tenders more competitive.

1.5.2 Adjudication and selection of the contractor

Assuming that the code of procedure for single-stage selective tendering is followed, the priced bills of the lowest contractor should be checked by the quantity surveyor. If any errors are found then these are reported to the architect, who in conjunction with the client (employer) determines what action is to be taken. This action should follow one of two options that should be stated in the preambles of the bills of quantities and the form of tender.

Option 1

The tenderer is given details of the errors and asked if he wishes to confirm or withdraw his offer. If the tenderer withdraws, the same procedure is followed with the second lowest tenderer. If the tenderer confirms his offer then an endorsement is added to the priced bills to the effect that all prices are to be considered as reduced or increased in the same proportion as the corrected total of priced items exceeds or falls short of such items. This adjustment excludes preliminary items, contingencies, prime cost and provisional sums.

Option 2

The tenderer is given an opportunity to confirm his offer or amend it to correct genuine errors. If the offer when amended is no longer the lowest, the next lowest tenderer should be considered. If the tenderer confirms his offer an endorsement will be required as in option 1.

Negotiated reduction of tender

It may be that the lowest tender under consideration exceeds the employer's budget, in which case negotiations usually take place to secure a reduction by amending the specification or quantities.

1.6 THE OPPORTUNITY TO TENDER

With a comprehensive knowledge of the available market, contractual arrangements and tendering procedures, the management of a building company can endeavour to direct its efforts towards the most favourable opportunities to obtain work. Information relating to the profitability and resources employed on previous contracts is patently necessary to help decide which will be the most advantageous contracts, since not only must work be obtained but it must be capable of being carried out with the resources available and create a profit.

SELF-ASSESSMENT QUESTIONS

1. Discuss the market conditions in the construction industry during the past year bearing in mind the prevailing interest rates and government policy.

2. Calculate the change in relative importance of the following categories of work between 1983 and 1985 at current prices and at seasonally adjusted prices:

   (a) all new work;
   (b) all repair and maintenance work.

   Refer to *Housing and Construction Statistics* Table 1.

3. Distinguish between the following types of contractual arrangements and explain the circumstances in which they should be employed:

   (a) single-stage selective tendering;
   (b) serial contracts;
   (c) term contracts.

4. Assuming the *Code of Procedure for Single-Stage Selective Tendering* is followed, explain the options that may be adopted for dealing with any errors found in the priced bills of quantities of the lowest contractor at the tender stage.

2

ESTIMATING
PROCEDURE

CHAPTER OBJECTIVES

After studying this chapter you should be able to:

- appreciate the complex relationships involved in preparing a competitive tender;

- understand the need to use a logical and systematic procedure to ensure that the most accurate cost prediction possible is arrived at.

2.1 INTRODUCTION

Before discussing the procedure to be followed in preparing an estimate, it is necessary to be quite clear how a contractor incurs the cost of a contract and to have an appreciation of the functional organization of a building company. Some typical examples are now presented to illustrate these points.

Consider a cost analysis of a five-storey office block to the following brief specification. The building is to be of reinforced concrete construction with strip and column foundations, brick and block external cavity walls, asphalt roofing, aluminium windows with double glazing, and a good standard of finishes and services.

2.1.1 Typical cost analysis of a five-storey office block

Floor area $2000\,\text{m}^2$; tender date November 1983.

	£
1. Excavation and earthwork	12 500
2. Concrete work	196 000
3. Brickwork and blockwork	78 000
4. Roofing	9 000

	£
5. Woodwork	26 500
6. Structural steelwork	1 500★
7. Metal balustrading	1 000★
8. Metal windows and entrance doors	49 000★
9. Plumbing and mechanical engineering installations	190 000★
10. Electrical installations	95 000★
11. Lift installation	48 000★
12. Plastering and floor screeds	16 500
13. Acoustic suspended ceilings	36 000★
14. Granolithic and terrazzo floor finishes	2 500
15. Flexible vinyl floor finishes	21 000
16. Ceramic wall tiling	2 500
17. Glazing	19 500★
18. Painting and decorating	14 000
19. Drainage	6 500
20. External works	12 500
21. Preliminaries	125 500
22. Contingencies	35 000★★
Total cost	£ 998 000
Cost per m² of floor area	£ 499

★ Prime cost sums
★★ Provisional sum

A similar analysis may be prepared by estimators for every tender, thus providing an invaluable bank of data for use in approximate estimating.

2.1.2 Bill of quantities summary

These figures will appear in the usual bill of quantities (BOQ) summary as follows:

Summary	£
General conditions and preliminaries	125 500
Measured works section	397 500
Prime cost and provisional sums	475 000
Total carried to the form of tender	£ 998 000

Part of the preliminaries and measured works section will be carried out by the main contractor's own work force and will be priced in detail by the estimator. The remaining work in these sections will be executed by subcontractors selected by the contractor. The bill of quantities summary shows that approximately half the cost is made up of prime cost and provisional sums—these figures are beyond the control of the main contractor.

For an analysis of the figures to determine how much work will be carried out by the main contractor's work-force, it is necessary to abstract and present the information as explained in the final chapter.

2.1.3 Management services and responsibilities

The ways in which construction companies are organised are as varied as the type and size of the work they carry out, and the diversity of character of their executives. However, most firms are organized on functional lines and an example of one such pattern of organization is given in Fig. 2.1. In building firms the departmental heads are often executive directors, and they constitute the board which decides the overall policy of the company. The company illustrated has been envisaged as being sufficiently large to employ all the specialist personnel listed, and can tender for a fairly large and complex project. If the company was much smaller the same activities would still have to be carried out, albeit on a much smaller scale; more than one function would then be performed by each member of staff.

Table 2.1 indicates the co-operation that is essential between the various functions to produce an effective tender. It should be appreciated that if such a schedule, or programme is prepared it will greatly assist in the preparation of the estimate within the tendering period.

2.1.4 Procedure for estimating and tendering

This is outlined in Table 2.1. The tendering period (greater than 25 working days) is based on a large contract. Actual tendering periods can vary from four to ten weeks or more, depending on the size and complexity of the contract. The activities concerned with 'the decision to tender' and 'the collection of information' will now be considered, with the remaining activities being dealt with in later chapters.

2.1.5 The decision to tender

It can readily be appreciated from a study of the activity schedule in Table 2.1 that the whole estimating and tendering process is a very costly business, involving probably many members of staff for several weeks—thus the decision to tender cannot be taken lightly. Such factors as the amount of work in hand, the work load for the estimating staff and the suitability (probable profitability) of the contract should be considered before a decision to tender is made. This is particularly the

Table 2.1 An activity schedule

Activity	Personnel	Day
Decision to tender		1
Receive invitation	E	
Scrutinize documents	E, QS	
Examine construction work load	CM	
Examine estimating work load	E	
Accept or decline	MD	
Collection of information		2–15
Programme estimate	E	
Check contract conditions	QS	
Materials enquiries	B or E	
Subcontract enquiries		
Visit site	E, SM, P	
Visit architect/consulting engineers		
Method statement	P, PM, SM, E	
Pre-tender construction programme		
Design temporary works	TWE	
(Formwork, gantries, crane bases, upholding sides of excavations, etc).		
Preparation of estimate		10–23
Calculate all-in labour rates	E	
Check material quotations	B/E	
Calculate unit rates for own work	E	
Check subcontract quotations	B/E	
Add subcontract attendance costs	E	
Enter rates for own work and subcontract work in BOQ	E	
Calculate project overheads and preliminaries	E, SM	
Summary of bills	E	
Analysis of resources (final summary)	E	
Report to management	E	
The tender		24–25
Adjudication	★	
Final calculations	E, A	
Submission of tender	E, MD	

Personnel:

MD	Managing director	B	Buyer
CM	Construction manager	P	Planner
E	Estimator	PM	Plant manager
QS	Quantity surveyor	A	Accountant
SM	Site manager and/or contracts manager	TWE	Temporary works engineer

★   All personnel may be involved at this meeting particularly on important contracts

Other personnel involved (depending on the size of firm) are likely to be: Cost and bonus, safety officer, labour officer, marketing, work study officer.

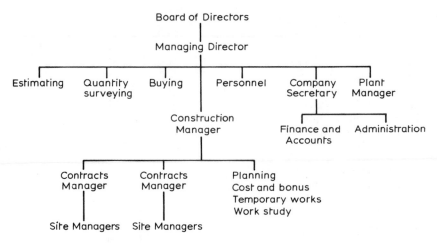

Fig 2.1

case when, as is usual, competitive tendering is employed and only one in five, or fewer, tenders are successful.

2.2 COLLECTION OF INFORMATION

On deciding to tender, the first urgent tasks are those concerned with the collection of information. Essentially, the tender documents are scrutinized again in a new light with the objective of deciding what further information is required to prepare the tender. The activities that ensue are now described with examples of appropriate check lists and records.

2.2.1 Programme estimate

The activity schedule may be translated into a programme, usually in bar chart form, to act as a guide to the responsibilities of the personnel involved in the preparation of the tender. Progress can also be checked at regular intervals to ensure that the tender is completed in the very limited time available.

2.2.2 Checking tender documents

The tender documents should be checked for completeness, and any onerous contract conditions should be noted for later consideration. An enquiry record should be completed as shown in Fig. 2.2.

Enquiry Record No. _86/30_

Title _Hypothetical Project_

General description _Three storey office_
block - R.C. construction with brick facings

Location _____ _Otley_
Date received _16 April 86_
Tender date _____ _21 May 86_

Client _____ _Complex PLC_
Architects _____ _Right Angle and Partners_
Quantity surveyor ____ _Measure and Cost Advice_
Consultants _____ _Structural and Services Associates_

Contract   _J.C.T. 80 Private with Quantities_

Appendix insertions:

Date of possession ___ _18 June 86_ _____ Date for completion _14 June 87_
Defects liability period ___ _6 months_ _____ Professional fees % _3_
Liquidated and ascertained damages _£500 per week_
Period of interim certificates ___ _monthly_ _____ Retention % _3_
Period of final measurement &
   valuation _____ _6 months_
Fluctuations alternative ___ _Firm price - clause 38_

Value of prime cost and provisional sums   £
   Nominated subcontractors .... 295 000 . 00
   Nominated suppliers .... 1 900 . 00
   Provisional sums   }   35 000 . 00
   Contingencies   —
   Total   331 900 . 00

Comments   _Approximate value £822 000_
           The largest comparable contract to this is No. 24 - £660 000
           Contract period 11 months. A check should be made on the
           financial commitment. This is however our type of work and we
           have worked well with the Architects and Consultants in
           the past.

                              ACCEPT/~~DECLINE~~ TENDER INVITATION

                              signed _J. Bentley_ ....

Fig 2.2

2.2.3 Fluctuations

One of the conditions to be made clear to suppliers and sub-contractors and which must be borne in mind by the estimator is whether the price has to be firm or will the effect of inflation be reimbursed by the client in some way. The operable clause is noted in the Appendix to the conditions of contract and stated in the bills of quantities.

The use of the term 'fixed price contract', in the context of fluctuations, should be avoided as this refers to either a lump sum, or measurement contract where the price(s) is/are fixed in relation to the lump sum or schedule of prices. A fixed price contract may be subject to any of the three alternative methods of dealing with fluctuations. Clause

37 of the *JCT Standard Form of Building Contract* refers to these three alternative methods, in accordance with the following clauses:

(a) *Clause 38.* Contribution, levy and tax fluctuations (limited fluctuations). If clause 38 is used, then any increases or decreases in contribution, levy and tax fluctuations shall, as the case may be, be paid to or allowed by the contractor. Since all other increases in the cost of labour and materials have to be borne by the contractor, where this condition applies, the contract is sometimes called a 'firm price contract', but more correctly is a contract with 'limited fluctuations'.

(b) *Clause 39.* Labour and materials cost and tax fluctuations (basic price list). If clause 39 is used, then, in addition to the adjustments for tax fluctuations, etc., specified in Clause 38, the contractor is reimbursed for any increase in wages and other emoluments and expenses promulgated after the Date of Tender by the National Joint Council for the Building Industry. Also, increases or decreases in the market price of materials or goods specified in a basic price list submitted by the contractor and attached to the Contract Bills shall, as the case may be, be paid to or allowed by the contractor. This is a very traditional method and is very laborious in operation.

In both the previous clauses a percentage addition to fluctuation payments or allowances is to be stated in the Appendix to the Contract. This percentage may be already filled in by the architect and may be any percentage including nil. In this event the contractor should include any anticipated shortfall in costs in the preliminaries or elsewhere.

(c) *Clause 40.* Use of price adjustment formulae. The application of this clause is governed by the provisions of this clause and the current Formula Rules issued by the Joint Contracts Tribunal. The value of work included in interim certificates is divided into work categories and the values are adjusted in accordance with the variation in the relevant NEDO Work Indices related to the month prior to date for receipt of tender (base month). In the local authority form, the amount of the increases is reduced by a 'non-adjustable element' of 10%. Thus the contractor only recovers 90% of any increase in the adjustment. Far less paperwork is involved in this method and, overall, seems more satisfactory than the adoption of clause 39.

Fluctuations and the tender

Patently the application of these clauses affects the amount of money, if any, that the contractor receives to compensate for the effect of inflation. Thus, the estimator must understand these clauses and get relevant advice of the effect of these clauses. Essentially the effect is as follows:

(a) *Clause 38.* Limited fluctuations. All future increases except for statutory increases must be allowed for by the estimator. Since in the past inflation has exceeded 25% per annum, very large sums may be involved, and if proper provision is not made large losses can occur with consequent probable insolvency. Limited fluctuation contracts are usually confined to contract durations of less than 12 months, but may be much longer.

Comments:

The material price increases are often calculated on a straight line basis, as an average for all materials, and on the assumption that purchases are made for the total period of the contract. In fact there may be known increases for particular materials at a certain date and also the bulk of the materials may be purchased well before the completion of the contract. In order to take these factors into account some form of programme/budget should be prepared, and utilized, to make a more accurate prediction of increased costs. It is unlikely, though possible, that material suppliers will give firm prices. An addition may be required for additional overheads and project margin, due to the increased costs. An example of the application of the above is given in the final chapter.

(b) *Clause 39.* Fluctuations in traditional method. Since labour increases are confined to the work force, and staff employed on site are classified as craftsmen for the purposes of calculating relevant increases, then account must be taken of any greater foreseeable expense. Material increases are confined to those materials on the basic price list and therefore any other probable material increases should be taken into account. Increases in general office overheads should also be considered as, for a contract of a long duration, they could be considerable. The cost of all the considerable necessary paperwork and calculations must also be taken into account.

(c) *Clause 40.* Fluctuations in formula method. This method is designed to simplify the calculations and adjust prices to cope with average increases. One important point is that overheads and profit automatically increase as the cost increases, so no further allowance need be made for this in the tender. The estimator has to consider if the contract increases are likely to be in line with the average increases and whether the contractor is likely to recover more or less than the actual increases by the application of the formula method. Dr. Martin Barnes, the pioneer of this method, has stated that, in a comparison made between actual increased costs, and increased costs calculated by the formula method, in two cases out of three there was a variation of ± 15%.

2.2.4 Enquiries to suppliers

Enquiries may be sent to builders' merchants who stock and supply an immense variety of materials such as: acoustic tiles, adhesives, barrows, cast iron pipes and fittings, damp course materials, expanded metal lathing, fireplaces... to zinc sheets. However, where full loads are required, such as aggregates or bricks, enquiries are usually sent direct to the suppliers.

In any event it is necessary to obtain competitive quotations (prices) from several suppliers wherever possible. To avoid undue expense on the part of the suppliers, quotations should not normally be requested from more than say four suppliers for the same material or product. The enquiries should state:

- site address;
- any delivery restrictions/traffic conditions/access problems;
- material description and specification;
- quantity and delivery programme;
- form of sub-contract to be employed;
- date by which the quotation is required;
- conditions of purchase.

It will often be preferable to photocopy the relevant specification requirements from the bills of quantities or specification and include these with the enquiry. Unnecessary handling, storage on site and waiting for deliveries should be avoided if at all possible. Thus the service provided by the builders' merchant should be taken into account when deciding which quotation to use in the tender, since the builder is concerned with the lowest cost fitted rather than the lowest cost delivered.

2.2.5 Enquiries to sub-contractors

These enquiries are more complex than those sent to suppliers since fixing is involved. Consequently the presence on site of sub-contractors' personnel and perhaps machines is required. Thus the following additional points should be stated:

- plant and other facilities to be provided by the main contractor;
- form of sub-contract to be employed;
- contract conditions as stated in the appendix such as terms of payment and applicable fluctuations clause.

The quotations when received should be summarized to determine which is the cheapest that meets all the requirements. The following headings would be appropriate in such a summary:

- Name of sub-contractor;
- Sub-contractor's conditions/qualifications;
- Plant/scaffold/special requirements;
- Quotation amount;
- Discount;
- Firm price allowance (if required and not included in quotation);
- Total amount included in BOQ.

Chapter Nine provides a more detailed study of sub-contractors' conditions and requirements together with reference to nominated sub-contractors.

2.2.6 Site visit

A visit should always be made to the site, and relevant information noted regarding factors affecting the methods of carrying out the work or the pricing of the project overheads. A pro-forma, similar to the one shown in Fig. 2.3, is usually used to act as a check-list and so that the information is presented in a logical and clear manner. In this example it has been assumed that the pro-forma is being used by a firm working within a short distance of its office. Where the work is carried out over a much wider area, other relevant information may be required, such as: details about labour availability, associated costs of bonus rates, lodging facilities and expenses; names and addresses of local material suppliers, sub-contractors and plant hire companies.

2.2.7 Visit architect and consulting engineers

General arrangement drawings are now issued with the tender documents. However further drawings are usually available for perusal at the architect's and consultant's offices. They can be helpful in determining how parts of the building may be assembled and constructed, and may indicate probable influences on cost.

2.3 PRE-TENDER PLANNING

2.3.1 Liaison meetings

These will be necessary between specialist staff to determine: construction methods, a site layout, a pre-tender construction programme, and proposed site staffing.

The pricing of excavation and concrete work cannot proceed until the methods have been determined. These will involve the selection of the most suitable types of mechanical and non-mechanical plant, the sequence of construction and, if at all possible, selection of gang sizes.

Site Visit Report

Project ...Hypothetical project...... Date of visit ..20 April 86......

1. Location ..Otley...

2. Transport services .Excellent bus service – no trains..............

3. Local Authority ..Leeds..

4. Access:

   to site .....roads to three sides..................................

   temporary roads ..not required.................................

5. Site description:

   contours ....slight slope..................................

   obstructions ...demolished housing, site well cleared........

   weather conditions ....

6. Ground conditions:

   strata ....clay subsoil...............................

   earthwork supports ..to be ascertained......................

   water: surface ....see site investigation report, depth........

           pumping/disposal unlikely to be a problem

7. Tip .....6 km – charge £ 1.20 per load.............................

8. Services:

   drainage .....adjacent.......................................

   water ....✓...

   gas ....✓...

   electricity .....✓...

   telephone ....✓...

9. Security requirements:

   hoarding ..2 m high plywood or similar.....................

   compound ...not required....................................

   watchman ..check with security agency.....................

10. Any other relevant information .Traffic problem on market days.....
    ....Adequate room for offices and mixing plant on site.............

Fig 2.3

2.3.2 Construction methods

After the drawings and bills of quantities have been studied and a site visit made, the methods of construction can be determined by the construction staff and the estimator (with the aid of specialist advice if necessary). This may entail seeking the advice of hire companies as to plant capabilities and performance. In the case of temporary works such as earthwork supports, an engineer experienced in this kind of problem may be called upon to prepare an outline scheme at tender stage. This should give sufficient detail for the estimator to evaluate the risk, and price the relevant items. The estimator should always have a clear perception of how the work that he is pricing may be carried out in a practical and economical manner.

Ideally *method statements* should be prepared for each major operation to indicate the type of plant to be used, both mechanical and non-mechanical, and the composition of the labour force (see example in Table 2.2). If, in addition, appropriate outputs are inserted, then the duration can be calculated. The same figures may then be used for preparing the construction programme and the estimate. The estimator must however satisfy himself that these outputs take into account, as far as possible, all the circumstances of the project, with due allowance for such factors as 'standing time'.

Table 2.2 Method statement and programme calculation sheet

CONTRACT Hypothetical project		TENDER No. 86/30			DATE DUE 20 April '86		
No. Operation	Quantity	Method/Plant	Gang	Output*	Duration (days)	Remarks
Excavation						
1 Reduced level	480 m³	B100 Drott with banksman	+1 L	12 m³/hr	5	
2 Foundation trenches	72 m³	JCB 3c with banksman	+1 L	3 m³/hr	3	
Disposal						
3 Spread and level on site	516 m³	Carried out at same time at item 1	—	—	—	
4 Backfill	24 m³	By hand	3 L	0.5 m³/hr	2	

* Outputs are for one machine or one man.

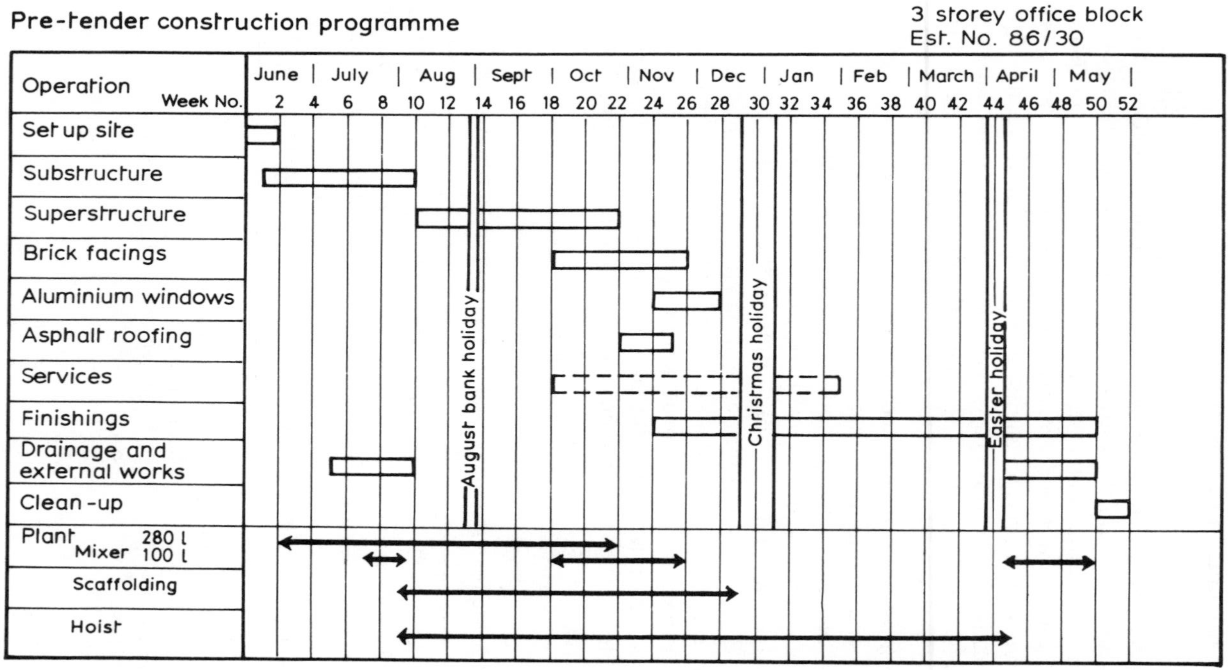
Pre-tender construction programme
3 storey office block
Est. No. 86/30
Operation
Week No.
June | July | Aug | Sept | Oct | Nov | Dec | Jan | Feb | March | April | May |
2 4 6 8 10 12 14 16 18 20 22 24 26 28 30 32 34 36 38 40 42 44 46 48 50 52
Set up site
Substructure
Superstructure
Brick facings
Aluminium windows
Asphalt roofing
Services
Finishings
Drainage and external works
Clean-up
Plant Mixer 280 l 100 l
Scaffolding
Hoist
August bank holiday
Christmas holiday
Easter holiday

Fig. 2.4

2.3.3 Site layout

The site layout is part of the method statement, and is usually drawn on the site plan indicating such features as:

- temporary services;
- hoardings and fencing with position of gates;
- temporary offices, including areas for sub-contractors' accommodation;
- canteen and welfare facilities;
- stores and material storage areas;
- temporary roads and access;
- hoisting facilities, including the radius of any cranes;
- scaffolding and fans;
- position of any temporary spoil heaps.

Site staff schedule   Est 86/30

Contract ...Hypothetical.........		Duration...52 weeks......	
Site staff	No.	Weeks required	Remarks
Site manager	1	52	? transfer W.S.B. from 85/13
General foreman	—		
Foreman Carpenter	1	18	Formwork
Bricklayer	1	8	Facings externally
Finishings	1	24	
Site engineer	1	22	
Chainman	1	22	} 50% of time
Checker/storekeeper	1	27	
Canteen attendant }	1	50	
Cleaners }			

Since this is a very large contract to be carried out in only 52 weeks, check viability of employing a production controller on site.

Fig 2.5

This will enable the estimator to make any necessary measurements and assess the cost.

2.3.4 Pre-tender construction programme

The programme should show the sequence and phasing of the main sections of work and the contract period based on the optimum methods giving the lowest estimated overall cost (see Fig. 2.4).

Where, as recommended in the *Code of Selective Tendering Procedure*, the contract period is stated in the tender documents, and this is less than indicated in the draft programme, further consideration must be given to determine the best method of completing the contract on time. This will invariably mean extra cost. A critical path programme would be most useful since the activities that require a shorter duration would then be obvious, being on the critical path.

2.3.5 Site organization

The site organization necessary to supervise the work set out in the programme and method statements may be listed in a site staff schedule (see Fig. 2.5) and this will assist in pricing the project overheads.

SELF-ASSESSMENT QUESTIONS

---

1. A large firm of contractors has been invited to tender for a multi-storey block of offices in a town some one hundred miles from their office.

   Describe the tendering procedure that should take place, and explain the roles of the various members of staff involved within the firm. Use diagrams and examples as necessary to clarify your answer.

2. Prepare a site visit form suitable for use by a small contractor working within a radius of ten miles from base.

3. Explain why method statements are considered to be an essential aid to estimators.

4. A specialist estimating company offers to carry out the pricing of bills of quantities for £7.00 per £1000 of contract value, excluding prime cost and provisional sums.

   Make a judgment as to the advisability of employing this company, and give a recommendation to the management of a building firm given the following data:

   - Turnover: £6 million.
   - Proportion of prime cost and provisional sums to total contract values: 45%.

- It is calculated that the equivalent of two men spend their time involved in the tendering process at a cost of £15 000 per man year, including provision of office facilities and clerical assistance.
- All jobs are obtained by competitive tendering under the code of selective tendering procedure.

3

PREPARATION OF UNIT RATES

CHAPTER OBJECTIVE

After studying this chapter you should be able to:

- understand the terminology related to the preparation of unit rates;

- identify and analyse the cost elements of unit rates;

- adopt a systematic approach to pricing unit rates in the measured works section of bills of quantities.

3.1 COST ELEMENTS

It is necessary to break down descriptions of work items in bills of quantities or schedules of rates into their cost elements in terms of materials, plant and labour.

The cost of each element should be calculated in detail, and in every case is made up of two components:

Materials	: unit cost × quantity required
Plant	: hire rate × time required
Labour	: cost per hour × time required.

An analytical approach to making cost break-downs is essential, and it helps if the sequence given above is followed.

All calculations should be carefully set down and annotated as necessary so that:

- the calculations can be checked by another person;
- the calculations and assumptions made can be readily explained to senior management;
- the information may be used by, say, buying or production control.

3.2 MATERIAL ELEMENT

Material element costs involve unit cost and the quantities required. These are fully explained below.

3.2.1 Unit cost

The material unit cost should take into account all appropriate charges and discounts. The most common of these factors are described below.

The following is an example of a typical quotation from a supplier.

Quotation

20 mm North Yorkshire aggregate to BS 882 £5.90 per tonne delivered to site in 12 tonne loads. 2½% cash discount.

It will be noted that *delivery charges* have been included in the example above, as is the case in most quotations. Because many building materials are either very heavy or bulky and are often relatively cheap to produce, transport costs form a significant proportion of their overall price. Consequently, quotations will vary for sites in different locations. For example, the cost of concrete blocks may vary by as much as 33⅓%, depending on the distance of the site from the factory. Sometimes delivery charges are quoted separately. This practice may be due to trade custom, or the possibility that the contractor may wish to collect the goods himself.

Fragile items, such as sanitary fittings, may be delivered in *packages* or *crates,* and there may be a separate charge for these, or the cost of returning the crates at a later time might have to be allowed for.

Trade discounts apply particularly when there are standard price lists prepared by manufacturers or suppliers and when items may be sold direct to the public. For example, builders and plumbers may get, say, a 20% discount on the supply of sanitary fittings, when compared with the retail price to the general public.

Discounts may also be given for quantity. For example, internal flush doors:

1 only	basic price
2 to 5	less 15%
6 to 24	less 25%
25 to 100	less 33%

above 100: quantity discount to be negotiated.

A *cash discount* is often given by suppliers to encourage early settlement of accounts. A statement is sent to the contractor at the beginning of each month listing the invoices for materials or services supplied during the previous month. If payment is made by the end of the month, a settlement (cash) discount may be taken of usually 2½%. Not all suppliers give this discount.

3.2.2 Quantities required

As well as considering basic bulk quantities of materials we must also take into account; waste factors, damage, breakages, unloading methods, storage, etc.

The units used in material quotations are often different from those used in bills of quantities: hardcore is quoted for per tonne, yet is measured in cubic metres (over 250 mm thick); and bricks are quoted per 1000, yet are measured by the square metre stating the thickness of the wall. The necessary *conversion factors* may be obtained by calculation in the case of the number of bricks per square metre, if the brick size and the thickness of the mortar joints are known. But in the case of bulk items, such as hardcore and aggregates, the quantity required per unit depends on such factors as the mass of the material, which varies according to its characteristics, source of supply, moisture content, etc. The materials may therefore have to be investigated by specialist staff if the estimator is to have accurate information (in the case of our example: North Yorkshire aggregate 20 mm–10 mm 1 760 kg/m^3.) Obviously, the greater the quantities required, the more care must be taken in obtaining the conversion factor. An inaccurate assumption may affect the tender significantly.

Waste factors can also be important. There are various types of waste and the amount can be alarming, for example E.R. Skoyles and H.J. Hussey of the Building Research Establishment found that on one major housing project the bricks wasted above the normal allowance included in the tender were equivalent to about ten extra houses or, taking the housing programme overall, it would amount to about 15 000 dwellings.

The various types of waste can be classified as follows:

- *Stockpile waste*. This includes loss of materials into the ground, contamination of materials by soil, and surplus materials 'lost'. Stockpile waste applies to such materials as aggregates.
- *Deterioration*. This results from the effect of dampness, rain, and so on, on unprotected materials. This applies particularly to materials such as cement, plaster, plasterboard and pre-finished components.
- *Breakages and other damage*. The effect of mishandling materials when they are unloaded, being fixed, or when finally in position. This applies to materials such as sanitary ware, glass or pre-finished components.
- *Cutting waste*. Many materials are not supplied to exact requirements,

e.g. Some cutting on bricks is normal to maintain the bond. If a special bond is required or if the design does not take into account the size of the bricks, then extra cutting may be required.

- *Residue waste*. This consists of materials that are surplus to requirements, e.g. perhaps four litres of paint of a special colour used when the container holds five litres.

    Theft may also be significant in certain areas.

Subsidiary materials, such as the mortar required for brickwork, nails and glue for woodwork, and bolts for formwork, must not be neglected—they often form an important proportion of the total cost of an item. These subsidiary materials should be treated in the same way as main materials, i.e. quotations must be obtained and quantities and cost required per unit calculated. For example: the cost of mortar calculated per cubic metre, and multiplied by 0.065 cubic metre, to give cost of mortar required per square metre of one brick wall in 65 mm bricks in English bond.

3.2.3 Unloading, storage and protection

Materials such as aggregate and hardcore are usually delivered in tipping trucks and therefore no *unloading costs* are incurred. Most other materials have to be unloaded, and a choice of unloading methods exists.

- Where materials are to be unloaded by hand it is most convenient to include the cost in the materials element, e.g. to unload common bricks add the cost for one hour of a labourer's time per 1 000 bricks to the delivered price. It is important to allow for the unloading costs before the addition of the waste allowance since this cost is incurred before the waste occurs.
- On a contract of any size the use of machines, such as rough terrain fork lifts and cranes of all types, should be considered. These machines may be used not only for unloading the materials, but for transporting them both horizontally and vertically—often positioning, say, precast concrete units in their final position. Furthermore, since the machines are often handling a variety of materials, it may be impracticable to allocate the cost accurately to particular materials. The cost of these machines is then included in the project overheads—not in the material rate.

    However, a careful check must be made by means of detailed calculations in association with the programme to ensure that the forklift, or other machine, can cope with the anticipated amount of unloading at the relevant times.

    A material may require to be banded or supplied on pallets to facilitate the use of machines, and there may consequently be an additional charge by the supplier.

- Suppliers' delivery vehicles often have a driver operated crane—Hiab or similar—and can unload the materials themselves without any assistance from the contractor. An additional charge is made for this service, say for bricks £2.50 per 1000. The bricks in this instance will be banded in packs to facilitate the use of the crane.

Valuable items, such as ironmongery, need to be kept in secure storage under the direct supervision of a storekeeper. Fragile items need to be protected from damage, and other items may need some protection from the elements by means of tarpaulins or other shelter. The cost of this is considered in project overheads, but a note must be made at the time of pricing of relevant items that appropriate storage or protection will be required so that the cost will not be forgotten.

3.3 PLANT ELEMENT

This is highly capital intensive and very large sums of money are involved. For example, in 1977 over £250 million of plant was bought, of which about one third was purchased by specialist plant hire companies.

On building sites the ratio of plant costs to labour costs is probably about 1:9, whilst on civil engineering contracts the ratio is often 1:1.

This ratio is changing, however, as more plant is being used on building sites every year due to:

- increased labour costs compared with plant costs;
- increased size of contracts;
- increased use of large components;
- greater speed of completion required; and
- the development of specialized building plant such as rough terrain fork lifts.

Consequently plant costs are assuming greater importance and more capital is required by building companies *if* plant is bought.

3.3.1 Methods of obtaining plant for contracts

There are *five* methods in general use for obtaining plant for contracts:

(a) buying it for the contract;
(b) hiring all the machines from a specialist hire company;
(c) having a pool of machines (Plant Department) and hiring some of the machines;
(d) leasing from manufacturers or bankers;
(e) sub-contracting.

The merits, or otherwise, of the above methods will now be looked at in more detail.

(a) Buying the required machines demands a large amount of capital, and, since depreciation rates are very high, this method is really only reasonable for big contracts of long duration. It is also very difficult for an estimator to predict the true cost under these circumstances, and thus make adequate, yet competitive, allowances in the tender.

(b) Hiring all the machines from a specialist hire company has many advantages. For example, no capital is required, and the capital thus released can be used to finance a greater volume of construction work. Further there is not the distraction of running a plant department with all its attendant problems, including finding and training plant operators and allowing for the cost of plant standing idle waiting for work. Generally, the best type of plant to suit the contract can be hired. However, when the industry is very busy there will be problems of availability, since most plant will then be in great demand, and hire rates will be likely to increase in response to market conditions.

(c) Having a pool of machines (Plant Department) is the method most widely adopted by medium and large contractors where the plant that is going to be used for an optimum period of time (having adequate utilization) is owned, whilst those machines that are only used occasionally are hired. As a general rule it can be said that if an item of plant is going to be used for more than a year, then it is worth buying. The function of the Plant Department is to supply plant as and when required by the contracts. Due allowance must be made for the heavy costs of running a Plant Department, including those for the idle time of plant awaiting work from contracts.

   The internal plant hire charges may often be nett (excluding profit) since profit will be added to the total cost of all the resources used on a contract in the tender summary as explained in chapter 12.

(d) Leasing from manufacturers or bankers has not until recently been very common in the UK. It is now rapidly increasing in popularity, since it enables a contractor to acquire the use of costly items of plant by making payments out of revenue. The contractor is only bound to make payments for the term of the lease, which is however usually fairly long, commonly between three and five years, but can go up to ten years. It should be noted that the lessee (the contractor) has full possession and use of the specific asset (item of plant) on payment of specified amounts over a period, while the lessor retains ownership.

(e) Sub-contracting is an increasing trend, since the main contractor off-loads part of the work and some of the risk onto the sub-contractor. A good example is excavation work, where a sub-contractor will carry out all the machine work in excavating and carting away. Allowance may have to be made by the estimator for: hand work, upholding the sides of excavations and generally tidying up. It is therefore essential to specify exactly what is required of the sub-contractor, so that the main contractor is not faced with the 'awkward work' and consequent unforeseen expense.

3.3.2 Methods of charging plant to contracts

Whether the plant employed on a site originates from company-owned sources or from independent plant hire companies, the following methods of charging for different items of plant will usually apply.

- Mechanical plant, such as excavators or cranes, are commonly called *operated plant* and include the cost of an operator and are hired at £x per hour (excluding fuel costs) with a minimum hire period, usually four hours.
- Mechanical plant such as compressors, concrete mixers, pumps and vibrators are classified as *non-operated plant*, and are hired by the week.
- Non-mechanical plant including such diverse items as site offices, scaffolding, adjustable trench struts and system formwork may be hired by the week or four-weekly period.
- Small items of equipment, such as picks, shovels and wheelbarrows, are usually charged on a pre- and post-contract valuation, sometimes known as an *on and off basis*. This method entails charging the contract with the cost of the items when sent to the site, and giving a credit when they are returned to the plant department. Often, of course, these items are lost or damaged, and the usual credit is 50% of the initial cost if returned in good condition. There is an incentive here for site management to take care. It is impracticable for an estimator to allow for the cost in such a manner, and a practical method is to relate the cost of these small items of equipment purchased per year to the labour cost per year as a percentage. This percentage is then multiplied by the labour cost included in tenders to arrive at the anticipated expenditure on such items. This sum is subsequently included in the project overheads.

3.3.3 Calculation of hire rates

Essentially any method of calculating hire rates must recover the cost of the plant over its expected useful life, and allow for the cost of the capital invested. There are many complications, such as the consequences of buying plant at different times and increased cost (inflation) giving different calculations for the same type of plant. It is impracticable to have different hire rates for, say, ten concrete mixers of the same size purchased over a period of time, and their rates are therefore averaged; this means that the plant hire rates must be constantly revised—usually every year. Further, this is essentially an area where the expertise of the cost accountant must be applied. There are many cost factors that should be considered when calculating the hire rates for mechanical and non-mechanical plant; not all factors are of course applicable to all categories. The following is a check list that applies to operated plant:

- initial capital cost;
- residual value at end of economic life;
- interest and service charges on the investment;
- taxation allowances; initial and annual;
- maintenance and repair costs;
- insurances;
- road fund licence if operated on a public highway;
- plant department overheads;
- fuel and other consumable items;
- operator's costs.

Table 3.1 is an example of a typical plant hire rate calculation that takes the above factors into account.

3.3.4 Allocation of plant costs

The calculation of plant cost elements will be considered in detail later. However, the following general points can be made here.

Where plant is used on specific items of work, and where the time required is directly related to the quantities of work, the estimated cost can be allocated to relevant units in the bills of quantities, as in the case of excavating plant. Where plant is used intermittently and/or on a number of different trades or operations—for example a crane being used for concrete, formwork and reinforcement distribution—then any allocation in the unit rates would be very complicated and arbitrary. Thus it is usual to include such costs in the project overheads. Alternatively, if the machine is used exclusively for one trade section in the bill of quantities, a lump sum may be included under 'Maintain on site all plant required for this section of the work.'

3.4 LABOUR ELEMENT

The total cost to a contractor of employing an operative is governed by the National Working Rules for the Building Industry, applicable Statutory Regulations and the scarcity, or otherwise, of particular trades. These factors will now be discussed in more detail.

Table 3.1 Example of plant hire rate calculation

Description of plant: Drott B100 (with 4-in-1 bucket and cab). Machine to be purchased by plant Department, and kept for three years.

Cost factors			£	Explanatory notes
Fixed costs				
Manufacturer's price delivered			16500	
HP interest 12% × 3 years		= 36%	5940	1
Maintenance 15% × 3 years		= 45%	7425	2
			29865	
Less resale value (trade-in)			2500	3
			27365	
Annual cost (÷ 3 years kept)			9122	4
Insurance (calculated on base price)		1%	165	5
Plant Dept. overheads		10%	1650	6
			10937	
Hourly cost				
Machine @ 1500 hours utilization			7.29	7
Running costs				8
Fuel: diesel	6 litre	0.30	1.80	
Lubricating oil and grease	10% of last		0.18	
Operator				
including allowance for: plus rates,				
travelling time, and off-hire time			4.50	
Daily maintenance $\dfrac{1 \text{ hour per day}}{8 \text{ hour working day}}$		@ 4.50	0.56	9
	All-in operating rate/hour		£14.33	10

Explanatory notes

1. This cost can represent either the interest on capital invested or hire-purchase interest.
2. The maintenance costs can be found by keeping cost records for each type of machine and representing the expenditure per annum as a percentage of the purchase price.
3. The re-sale or trade-in value can only be assessed at the current rate, and varies considerably depending on the demand for second-hand machines.
4. The annual cost has been based on the straight-line method of depreciation. This of course is not strictly accurate, and therefore a loss would be incurred if the machine had to be sold before the anticipated time. However, if the machines are normally kept for the anticipated period, this is a satisfactory method and has the advantage of simplicity.
5. The plant should be insured for all risks of loss or damage.
6. Plant Department overheads include the cost of administration and the workshops and plant yard.
7. Utilisation hours represent the time hired out to sites and charged for, and include any idle time on site. Patently the greater the number of hours the plant can be hired to site, the lower the hourly cost will be.

3.4.1 The national working rules for the building industry (NWR)

These rules are agreed by the National Joint Council for the Building Industry. This body consists of representatives of the Building Employers' Confederation, formerly known as the National Federation of Building Trades Employers, and the participating unions, consisting at the present time of the Union of Construction and Allied Trades and Technicians, the Transport and General Workers Union, the General and Municipal Workers Union and the Furniture Timber and Allied Trades Union.

It will be noted that not all trades are parties to the National Working Rules (NWR); electricians, plumbers, heating and ventilating engineers, and other operatives who are employed by specialist sub-contractors have their own negotiating machinery and agreements.

The main functions of the Joint Council are to fix the rates of wages of building trade operatives and to determine conditions of employment in the building industry. The National Working Rules lay down agreed principles. However, within this framework there are numerous regional or area variations (nationally approved), which in practice need to be ascertained.

(There is a similar agreement concerning civil engineering work, however the principles are the same.)

It is recommended that a current copy of the rules is obtained and consulted when preparing estimates, since amendments and revisions are constantly being made.

Reference to particular rules affecting costs will be made when those costs are calculated. A working knowledge of the rules is, however, required when estimating, since such diverse matters as working hours, guaranteed weekly wages, extra payments to labourers for operating concrete mixers and other mechanical plant, overtime rates, holiday payments and travelling allowances are all contained in the rules and need to be taken into account.

3.4.2 Statutory requirements

The following types of expenditure are incurred in complying with Acts of Parliament and the regulations they lay down relating to employment.

---

8. Fuel costs are usually excluded if the machine is hired externally.
9. One hour per day of the operator's time has been allowed for daily maintenance, to be worked outside normal working hours. This servicing is paid for at 'plain-time' rates.
10. This all-in operating rate represents the direct cost to the Plant Department. This figure may be affected by two further considerations:
    (a) an allowance for profit margin; and
    (b) the effect of taxation allowances which could reduce the effective cost.

The Employers' Liability (Compulsory Insurance) Act requires that all employers must insure against liability for personal injury and absence sustained by their employees arising out of their employment.

The Employment and Training Act is designed to secure an improvement in both the quality and quantity of training, and to provide for a fair distribution of the cost of training amongst employers. The Construction Industry Training Board was set up by the Secretary of State for Employment under this act to encourage training in the industry and to initiate courses if necessary. The CITB has a Plant Operatives' Training Centre at Bircham Newton, and runs general Safety Training Centres throughout the country. To pay for the cost of training the CITB is empowered to impose a levy on employers and the current rates are: craftsmen £75.00 per annum; labourers £18.00 per annum.

The Redundancy Payments Act provides for redundancy payments to be made in relation to the age of the employee and the number of years employed; for example, one week's pay per year of employment when the employee is between the ages of 22 and 40 inclusive. There are various qualifications as to what constitutes a week's pay and there is also a maximum amount to be considered. Further, employees must have a minimum of two years continuous service with an employer to qualify for payment.

Redundancy payments are payable by the employer who may, however, claim a rebate from the Department of Employment of 41%.

Under the terms of the National Insurance Social Security Act, national insurance contributions from employees and employers are collected, along with income tax under the PAYE procedure.

3.4.3 All-in hourly labour rates

It is convenient for an estimator to calculate labour costs based on the all-in hourly rates. Some examples are given below which should be studied in relation to the previous paragraphs and the explanatory notes following the calculations.

The all-in hourly rate is a very complicated calculation. Many of the relevant factors to be taken into account are subject to frequent changes. It is important that forthcoming changes and amendments to rules and regulations should be considered, and that the accountant responsible for the compilation of wages sheets (pay-roll) should be consulted to help in this matter and to check the calculations.

Because so many of the costs are fixed costs per year or do not apply to every week, the total cost of employing an operative per year should be calculated. This cost can then be divided by the number of productive hours to give the all-in hourly labour rate.

The example of a calculation of all-in labour rates (Table 3.2) takes the above factors into account. The calculation is based on a standard working week of 39 hours and the guaranteed minimum bonus payment.

Table 3.2 Calculation of all-in labour rates from 30 June 1986

Labour Charges		Craftsmen £	Labourer £	Notes
Taxable pay per week				
Standard basic grade A wages		98.280	83.85	1
Guaranteed minimum bonus		15.21	12.87	2
Guaranteed minimum weekly earnings		113.49	96.72	
Rate per hour (weekly rate ÷ 39) =		2.91	2.48	
Taxable pay per year				
Hours available for work				
1698 × rate		4941.180	4211.040	3
Working rule allowance				
$\frac{1698}{39} = 43.54$ W @ 1.12		48.765	—	4
Holidays with pay				
Annual	47 W @ 12.50	587.500	587.500	5
Public	63 hrs @ rate	183.330	156.240	6
		5760.775	4954.780	
Non-taxable charges				
National insurance	9%	518.470	445.930	7
Contractors insurance	2%	114.215	99.096	8
Sick pay allowance		44.000	44.000	9
Training levy		75.000	18.000	10
		6513.460	5561.806	
Severance pay allowance	1.5%	97.700	83.427	11
Annual cost per operative		6611.162	5645.233	
Divide annual cost per operative				
by productive hours	1634	4.046	3.455	
All-in rate per hour	say	4.05	3.45	

Explanatory notes to Table 3.2

1. Standard basic grade A rates of wages and guaranteed minimum bonus payments are as NWR 1. London and Liverpool District payments are slightly higher.
2. An incentive bonus scheme may be operated in place of the guaranteed minimum bonus. The average bonus paid in the construction industry, according to recent Department of Employment statistics was 30%. It will be appreciated, however, that this is a highly variable factor according to circumstances.
3. The calculation of hours available for work and productive hours makes allowance for inclement weather time that is paid for, but during which there is no production.

Based on a working week of 39 hours: Mon/Thurs 8 hour day; Friday 7 hour day.

Hours available for work = 52 weeks × 39 = 2028 hours.

less

21 days annual holiday		
16 days @ 8 hours		128
5 days @ 7 hours		35
8 days Public Holiday		
7 days @ 8 hours		56
1 day @ 7 hours		7
6 days assumed sick @ 8 hours		48★
7 days assumed absent @ 8 hours		56★
		330 hours

2028 − 330 = 1698 hours

less

Time lost due to inclement weather
Average 8 days @ 8 hours   64★
Productive hours = 1698 − 64 = 1634

4. The working rule allowance of £1.12 is for tool money and varies for different trades, see NWR 18.
5. The annual holiday with pay stamp is currently £12.50 per week operative from 4th August 1986. This includes a contribution to the Building and Civil Engineering Retirement and Death Benefit Scheme.
6. An allowance has to be made for paying the operatives one day's pay, based upon guaranteed minimum weekly earnings, for each day of public holiday.
7. The National Insurance contribution payable by the employer is at present 9% on employees' total earnings below £139.99 per week. On total earnings of £140.00 as more the percentage is 10.45.
8. The premium for contractors' insurance (employers' liability third party insurance) varies with the type of work being undertaken by the contractor and his claims record.
9. Sickness and injury payments are payable under NWR 16. In this example it has been assumed that cover is being provided by an insurance company for the premium indicated.
10. The training levy is payable to the construction industry training board.
11. The severance pay allowance is intended to cover the cost of redundancy benefits and associated costs when an operative is discharged.

★ The hours lost due to sickness, absenteeism and inclement weather time may be obtained from an analysis of the pay roll accounts and cost records.

All-in labour rates used in this book

Since a period of time has elapsed between these calculations being made and the publication of this book, the following rates have been used here:

Craftsmen   £4.60 per hour.
Labourers   £3.90 per hour.

Attendance on craftsmen

Craftsmen usually require labourers to fetch and carry for them and to provide general assistance. Since most work is carried out by gangs of men, the problem of allowing for the cost of this attendance can be

Table 3.3 Calculation of all-in labour rates from 30 June 1986

Labour charges			Craftsmen £	Labourers £
Taxable pay per week				
Standard basic grade A rates of wages			98.280	83.850
Incentive bonus		@ 33.1/3%	32.760	27.950
			131.040	111.800
Rate per hour	(weekly rate ÷ 39) =		3.36	2.867
Taxable pay per year	C	L		
Productive hours 1634	3.36	2.867	5 490.240	4 684.678
Inclement weather time 64	2.91	2.48	186.240	158.720
Working rule allowance as before			48.765	—
Holidays with pay				
Annual as before			587.500	587.500
Public as before			183.330	183.330
			6 496.075	5 614.228
Non-taxable charges				
National insurance		9%	584.647	505.280
Contractors' insurance		2%	129.921	112.285
Sick pay insurance			44.000	44.000
Training levy			75.000	18.000
			7 329.643	6 293.793
Severance pay allowance		1.5%	109.945	94.407
Annual cost per operative			7 439.588	6 388.200
Divide annual cost per operative by productive hours		1634	4.553	3.909
All-in rate per hour		say	4.55	3.91

overcome by including the labourers in the gang costs. Examples of this method are given in the following chapters.

Supervision

The additional cost of labour gangers, trades' foremen and chargehands may be allowed for when calculating gang costs, or may be allocated in the project overheads.

3.4.4 Incentive bonus

The calculation shown in Table 3.3 is similar to the previous example, but in this case it has been assumed that an incentive bonus of 33⅓% of the basic wage will be paid instead of the guaranteed minimum bonus.

It will be noted that during the anticipated period of inclement weather time, the men cannot earn bonus and will therefore fall back onto the guaranteed minimum bonus payments.

3.5 OUTPUT STANDARDS

3.5.1 Definition

Output standards are defined as the time allowances needed to carry out work under specific conditions; for example, 3.50 man hours are needed to excavate 1 m^3 of firm soil in a foundation trench not exceeding 2.00 m deep.

Many building firms record the cost of work on a trade basis, split down into operations or units; this is, in any event, required if an effective incentive scheme is operated. These cost records can then be used as the basis for estimating future performance, taking into account the relevant conditions applicable when the costs were recorded. The larger contractors have work study departments, and these can be of great help to an estimator, particularly in the case of unusual items where a very sophisticated system of building up times for work elements can be adopted using synthetics.

Other sources of information regarding outputs, such as manufacturers' literature for mechanical plant or system formwork, have to be treated with the utmost care since any figures that might be given tend to be very optimistic and do not usually allow for contingencies, relaxation time, etc.

Production standards are an alternative title for output standards. It will be appreciated that the use of the term 'constant' when referring to output standards can be most misleading when one considers the many variables involved. The use of this term should therefore be avoided.

3.5.2 Factors affecting outputs

There are three major groupings of factors affecting outputs.

(a) Factors that can be controlled by the contractor. The incentive to work, which is influenced by the level of incentives and morale, is an example of this type of factor. Other examples include: the balancing of gang sizes, so that the flow of work is not affected by the need to wait for other trades to complete their work; the provision of adequate crane or hoist facilities, so that the operatives are not held up due to a lack of materials; and the use of the most efficient construction method.

(b) Factors that cannot be controlled by the contractor. These are mostly design requirements, such as the quantity and complexity or otherwise of the work, the quality of finish, standard of workmanship, degree of accuracy required and the amount of repetition. The time of year when the work is to be carried out will indicate the likely seasonal conditions of weather and lighting.

(c) Factors that are only partly under the control of the contractor. These are mostly concerned with labour relations, such as the availability or otherwise of particular skilled tradesmen, and rates of absenteeism which can be very high.

In simple terms any task, such as building a brick wall, can be split into three phases: start; carry out the bulk of the work; and finish. Thus the larger the task the greater the average speed or productivity will be. Hence the average output from start to finish will be higher; the converse also applies. A learning phase may also be involved, so that as a gang of bricklayers build an increasing number of houses of the same design then, as they learn through experience, the number of bricks laid per hour should increase to an optimum.

It can be seen then that selecting the probable actual output requires the estimator to take all the available factors into account and co-relate them to output standards derived from previous contracts. This is one of the most difficult tasks that the estimator has to perform. Thus it will be appreciated that if a comparison is made between published output standards they will often be seen to vary greatly since they are based upon differing circumstances.

3.5.3 Direct unit rate format

As stated previously, it is essential that all calculations are set out in a

Table 3.4 Example of direct unit rate format

Item			Rate	Extension	Total
				Work section *brickwork and blockwork*	
Common bricks in cement mortar (1:3)					
4/5/C Foundation walls one brick thick in English bond					
Materials:				($£/m^2$)	
118	Common bricks				
		($£/1000$)			
	Delivered price	96.20			
	Unload: Labour 1 hr	3.90	100.10	11.812	
	Waste		5%	0.591	
$0.065m^3$	Cement mortar		56.08	3.645	
	(including waste)				
					16.048
Labour:					
65B/hr	$\dfrac{118}{65} = 1.815$ hours				
	Cost per gang hour	*£/hour*			
	2 Bricklayers @ 4.60	9.20			
	1 Labourer	3.90			
		13.10			
	Cost per bricklayer hour $\div 2 =$		6.55		11.888
					27.936
	Nett unit rate				27.94

clear and systematic form, and it is useful if the elements of materials, plant and labour can be kept separate so that the resource analysis in the final summary may be prepared.

Table 3.4 is an example of the direct unit rate format which is suitable for the simpler type of problem. Where the work is more complex, the indirect or operational unit rate format will be found to be easier to understand and will be more accurate.

The rate of £27.94 (usually rounded down to two decimal places) is then inserted in the rate column of the bills of quantities. Further, the individual rates for materials and labour can also be inserted in the general contractor's own copy, in order to prepare a resource analysis for the final summary for consideration by management.

Indirect (operational) unit rate format

Table 3.5 is an example of the indirect unit rate format.

Table 3.5 Indirect (operational) unit rate format

Item			Rate	Extension	Total
4/10/D	Hardcore, or the like Filling in making up levels over 250mm thick Deposited and compacted in layers of max. thickness 150mm				
		m^3			
	Quantity (from BOQ)	24			
	Compaction and waste 25%	6			
		30			
	@ 1500 kg/m^3 = 45t				
Materials			($£$/t)	($£$/24m^3)	
45t	Brick hardcore		6.00	270.00	
	Extra for 5t under full load		1.00	5.00	
				275.00	
Plant		($£$)	($£$)		
2 days	Wacker Rammer ⎫ Hire/day ⎬		6.00		
	Fuel/day 8 litres @ 0.30		2.40	8.40	16.80
Labour		*Gang*			
	Load barrow ⎱ Wheel 20m ⎰	1 @ 1	3.90	3.90 3.90	
	Spread and level	1		3.90	
	Compact	1	3.90 + 10p	4.00	
		4		15.70	
	Output 2½ MH/m^3 × 24m^3 = 60 MH ÷ 4 man gang = 15 gang hours (2 days)			15.70	235.50
					($£$/m^3)
	Nett rate/m^3 ÷ 24m^3			527.30	21.97

Note: The material can be tipped 20 metres from the fill area and the ground is firm and level. The hardcore is delivered in tipping trucks of 10 tonne capacity.

┌─────────────────────────────────────┐
│   SELF-ASSESSMENT QUESTIONS   │
└─────────────────────────────────────┘

1. Define the following factors, and explain how they should be taken into account when calculating the material element of unit rates:

   (a) cash, quantity and trade discounts;
   (b) conversion and waste factors.

2. (a) Prepare a check list of items that should be considered when calculating the hire rates for mechanical plant.
   (b) Using assumed figures, show how these factors are taken into account when calculating the hire rate for an excavator.

3. Using current data calculate the all-in hourly rates for both craftsmen and labourers working a basic week (no overtime) with an anticipated incentive bonus of 25%.

4

EXCAVATION AND EARTHWORK

CHAPTER OBJECTIVES

After studying this chapter you should be able to:

- appreciate the main factors that affect the cost of excavation and earthwork items;
- calculate representative examples.

4.1 CLASSIFICATION

The excavation and earthwork section in the Standard Method of Measurement (SMM) includes the following work:

- site preparation;
- excavation;
- earthwork support;
- disposal of water;
- disposal of excavated material;
- filling;
- surface treatments.

Examples are now given of the factors that should be considered and of calculations required to price this work.

4.2 GENERAL FACTORS

The following are some of the factors that may affect the cost of excavation and earthwork. The expected weather conditions can influence costs. The likelihood of rain may influence the type of excavator and haulage vehicles, and cleaning of adjacent roads may have to be allowed for, together with the provision of wheel-cleaning equipment. The type of material to be excavated and the water table can also affect costs. The harder the material the lower will be the output either by hand or machine, but it is less likely that it will be necessary to allow for upholding the sides of the excavation. Information may be available from a site investigation report prepared by the consulting engineers, from an examination of adjacent construction sites and, perhaps, from previous experience of working in the area.

4.3 EXCAVATION

4.3.1 Depths of excavation

Depths of excavation are classified as follows:

Maximum depth not exceeding 0.25 m;
Maximum depth not exceeding 1.00 m;
Maximum depth not exceeding 2.00 m;

and thereafter in 2 m stages.
    This depth factor is taken into account in the output standards.

4.3.2 Bulking of materials after excavation

Quantities are given in cubic metres as measured before excavating. Bulking must therefore be added and taken into account where necessary, e.g. in spoil heaps, or in the calculations for disposal of excavated material (Table 4.1).

Table 4.1 Bulking of materials after excavation

Material	% bulking
Gravel	10–20
Sand	12½
Earth	25
Clay	33⅓–50
Chalk	50–80
Rock	75–100

4.3.3 Output standards

Output standards during manual and mechanical excavation are elaborated in Tables 4.2 and 4.3.

Table 4.2 Output standards—excavation (by hand)

Excavating	Labourer (hours per m³)
Topsoil	2.00
Surfaces to reduce levels	
not exceeding 0.25 m deep	2.50
not exceeding 1.00 m deep	2.75
Basements; starting from reduced level	
not exceeding 2.00 m deep	3.25
not exceeding 4.00 m deep	4.75
Trenches: starting from reduced level	
not exceeding 1.00 m deep	3.00
not exceeding 2.00 m deep	3.50
Pits: starting from reduced level	
not exceeding 1.00 m deep	4.00
not exceeding 2.00 m deep	5.00
Disposal	
Back filling and compacting in layers	1.50
Remove surplus material a distance	
Not exceeding 50 m deposit	1.50
Spread, level and compact in	
150 mm layers	1.25
Load surplus material { into wheelbarrows	1.25
{ into trucks	1.75
Sundry labours	(hours/m²)
Level and compact bottom of excavation	0.10
Trimming, sloping face of embankment	
or cuttings	0.15
Strip turf, roll up and set aside	0.35
Relay turf, previously set aside	
including preparation and rolling	0.25

The excavation outputs given above are based on the ground being firm soil. For other materials, multiply the labour hours by the following factors:

Loose material	0.75
Gravel, loose chalk or stiff clay	1.50
Chalk–solid (needing a pick for removal)	2.50

Table 4.3 Output standards—excavation (by machine)

Machine	Standard bucket size (m³)	All in rate (£/hr)	Outputs (m³/hr)	
			Trench	*Bulk*
JCB 3c hydraulic excavator	0.20		3	5*
JCB 6c hydraulic excavator				
Hymac 580 hydraulic excavator }	0.50		9	15*
International B100 Drott	0.75		—	20*
Caterpillar 955	1.33		—	35*
Caterpillar 977K with ripper	2.30		—	50*
			Bulk excavation and disposal	
			50m	*100m*
International B100 Drott	0.75		12	8
Caterpillar 955	1.33		25	16
Caterpillar 977K	2.30		40	25
Caterpillar D8 bulldozer	—		32	20
		200m	*400m*	*600m*
Crawler scraper	4m³	—	14	10	8
Crawler scraper	8m³	29	20	16
Crawler scraper	12m³	45	31	26
Wheeled scraper	8m³	—	40	30

*Assumed bulk excavation loaded into trucks or other haul units.

Notes to Table 4.3
1. Excavation outputs above based on the ground being firm soil.
   For other materials multiply outputs by the following factors:

     Loose material   1.50
     Gravel, loose chalk or stiff clay 0.66
     Chalk–solid   0.50

     but bear in mind note 2.
2. The larger the machine the less it will be affected by the hardness of the material.
3. Variations in outputs of hydraulic excavators due to depth factor:

     Maximum depth not exceeding 0.25m × 0.50
     Maximum depth not exceeding 1.00m × 0.90
     Maximum depth not exceeding 2.00m × 1.00
     Maximum depth not exceeding 4.00m × 0.90

4. Remember that there is a limit to the depth any machine can dig.

4.3.4 Examples of typical unit rate calculations

Hand excavation

Note that the four items set out in Table 4.4 are taken to be in small quantities, and that it is therefore considered that the excavation will be undertaken by labourers (hand excavation). In this example, even though the quantity is small, it may be worth bringing in a machine. This may be particularly desirable due to the high labour content. Alternatively the use of a pneumatically operated spade should be considered in order to achieve a higher output, and a lower cost.

Table 4.4 Unit rate calculation for hand excavation

Item	Rate	Extension ($£/m^3$)	Total ($£/m^3$)
4.1 *Site preparation:* Preserving topsoil (D.9) Excavate average 100mm deep Information: Disposal separately; consider cost per m^3 then calculate rate for required thickness on a proportional basis Labour			
2 MH Labourer	3.90	7.80	
100mm thickness			0.78
4.2 *Excavation:* Excavating to reduce levels (D.13.3); maximum depth not exceeding 0.25m Information: Subsoil loose material Labour			
2.5 MH ×0.75 loose material			
1.875 labourer	3.90		
4.3 *Excavating trenches to receive foundations:* Starting from reduced level (D. 13.6) maximum depth not exceeding 1m. Information: Subsoil stiff clay Labour			
3MH normal excavation ×1.5 stiff clay			
4.5 labourer	3.90		17.55
4.4 *Maximum depth not exceeding 2m:* Information: Subsoil solid chalk 3.5 MH normal excavation n.e. 2m ×2.5 solid chalk			
8.75 labourer	3.90		34.12

Machine excavation

Wherever the quantities are sufficiently large, and it is practicable, machines will invariably be used since the cost will be less than that for hand excavation. The time taken will also be much reduced. At the beginning of the trade section in the BOQ there will be items for bringing plant onto site and maintaining plant on site. The method of pricing these two items is now illustrated, followed by three unit rate calculations using mechanical plant.

Bringing plant on to site (SMM item D4, plant)

An item shall be given for bringing to site, and removing from site, all plant required for this section of the work. For example:

Hydraulic tracked excavator	(JCB 6C)	
Required for bill items	4C/D/E	
and	6D/E/F	

	(£)
Quote for hauling to site on low loader from depot	226.00
Quote for taking off site	226.00
JCB 3C wheeled excavator Required for bill items... From external hire company's depot Hire charges for driving to site 4 hours @ 11.00	44.00
Hire charges for driving off site	44.00
Compressor 250 CFM Haulage to site	14.00
Haulage off site	14.00
	568.00

Maintaining plant on site (SMM item D4, plant)

An item shall be given for maintaining on site all plant required for this section of the work. For example:

On a general building site, where insufficient plant is used to justify a maintenance fitter being on site full time, it is usual for the hire rates for mechanical plant to include for all maintenance costs.

Daily maintenance is the responsibility of the operators and may take between half and one hour per day. The daily maintenance costs would be allowed here or in the all-in plant hire rate.

Table 4.5 Unit rate calculation for machine excavation

Item		Rate	Extension	Total
4.5	*Excavate basements and the like* starting from reduced level (D.13.4) Not exceeding 4m deep Information: Subsoil first 1 m firm soil. Thereafter stiff clay, to be excavated by hydraulic back actor with a 0.5m^3 bucket.			
	Machine	(£/hr)		
	Hymac 580 hire rate including fuel + operator	13.60		
	Banksman 3.90 + 0.10	4.00		
		17.60		
(m^3/hr)				
15.00	in firm soil not exceeding 2m deep			
13.50	not exceeding 4m deep × 0.9			
9.00	in stiff clay × 0.66			
(m)			(£/4m^3)	
	Thus rate calculation:			
1.00	depth in firm soil 1m^3 @ 13.50 m^3/hr	17.60	1.30	
3.00	depth in stiff clay 3m^3 @ 9.00 m^3/hr	17.60	5.87	
			7.17 (£/m^3)	
	Rate per m^3(★)			1.79
4.6	*Excavating trenches to receive foundations* starting from reduced level (D.13.6) *Maximum depth not exceeding 1m* Information: Subsoil firm soil, sufficient quantity to be excavated by small hydraulic back actor with 0.20m^3 bucket			
	Machine	(£/hr)		
(m^3/hr)	JCB 3c	11.00		
3.00	Banksman 3.90 + 0.10	4.00		(£/m^3)
× 0.9	as depth less than 2m			5.55
		15.00		
2.70				

Table 4.5 (*Contd.*)

Item		Rate	Extension	Total
4.7	*Maximum depth not exceeding 2m* Information: Subsoil stiff clay *Machine*			
(m³/hr) 3.00	JCB3C + Banksman as last	15.00		7.50
× 0.66 ——— 2.00	as stiff clay			

*The calculation illustrates how account may be taken of the reduction in anticipated outputs of the machine in digging material which is hard and at a depth below 2m. Care must be taken to ensure that the machine can dig to the required depth.

4.4 EARTHWORK SUPPORT (D14–D24)

4.4.1 Introduction

Earthwork support, formerly known and often still referred to as planking and strutting, is measured in square metres and classified by maximum depth as in excavation work. It is necessary to determine what, if any, support is required to the sides of the excavations and thus it is essential to visit the site, study conditions and site investigation reports if available. It may be necessary to obtain the specialist advice of a structural engineer to design the supports. A cross-section of typical earthwork support would be most helpful, enabling the necessary quantities to be measured for pricing.

Space to accommodate earthwork support (SMM item D10)

This states that no allowance shall be made for any extra space required to accommodate any earthwork supports, and thus if any additional excavation is required for this purpose the subsequent cost should be taken into account when pricing the relevant earthwork support items.

Earthwork support to additional excavation (SMM item D15 Id)

This states that earthwork support is not measured to the face of any additional excavation which results from the measurement of working space. This additional area is not usually significant except in the case of pits.

4.4.2 Output standards—earthwork support

The work (detailed in Table 4.6) may be undertaken by labourers who, in accordance with the National Working Rules, are paid a small additional sum per week for the extra skill and responsibility. Alternatively the work may be carried out by carpenters assisted by labourers.

The material cost is affected by the number of times timbers can be used before they are fit only for scrap: ten would be a normal figure for use on trenches, but probably far less in relation to timbers that are left in place a long time such as extensive basements. Some items, such as trench struts or proprietary supports, may be hired, and in this event time is all important and the programme requirements should be studied. The example given illustrates these last two factors of uses and time.

4.4.3 Example of earthwork support calculation

Maximum depth not exceeding 2m; distance between opposing faces not exceeding 2m.

Information: Ground conditions compact gravel and sand, trenches mostly 1.5m deep, support to consist of 50×150 poling boards at 600mm centres, 75×150 wales in three rows and adjustable trench struts at 2m centres along wales.

Consider then an average trench 50 metres long and 1.5m deep. Area $= 2/50 \times 1.5 = 150$ m^2.

Table 4.7 and 4.8 set out the material costs and the unit rate respectively.

Table 4.6 Output standards–earthwork support

Description	Unit	Man hours	Remarks
Timbers			The hours include time for normal hand-
Fix	m^3	12	ling and movement on
Strip	m^3	6	site.
Trench struts			
Fix	each	0.08	Allow ½ man hour
Strip	each	0.04	per m^3 for initial unloading of timber
Steel trench sheets			
Fix	m^2	0.20	
Strip	m^2	0.10	

Table 4.7 Materials

Description	Number	Length (m)	Cross-section (mm)	(m³)
Poling boards	$\dfrac{50\text{m}}{600\text{mm}} = 83 + 1 = 84$ $\times 2 \text{ sides} = \dfrac{168}{6}$	1.5	50 × 150	1.890
Wales	3 rows × 2 sides	50	75 × 150	3.375
				5.265
	Initial waste and sundries		10%	0.527
				5.792

Table 4.8 Unit rate calculation for earthwork support

Item		Rate	Extension (£/150m²)	Total
4.8 *Materials:* Trench struts $\dfrac{50\text{m}}{2} = 25 + 1 \times 3 \text{ rows} = 78 \text{ N}_o^y$				
		£/m³		
5.8m³ timber supply		187.85		
unload ½ hr 3.90		1.95		
		189.80	189.80	1100.84
divide by uses, say			÷ 10	110.08
nails, say			5%	5.50
				115.58
78 trench struts, say in use 2 weeks			0.15	23.40
				138.98
Labour	(MH)			
(5.8 m³)–Fix timber 12 hrs/m³	69.60			
(78) –Fix struts 0.08 hrs each	6.24			
(5.8 m³)–Strip timber 6 hrs/m³	34.80			
(78) –Strip struts 0.04 hrs each	3.12			
Timberman	113.76	4.00	455.04	(£/m²)
Labourer 3.90 + 0.10		÷ 150	594.02	3.96

You should note that the timber cost in Table 4.8 has been based on an average expectancy of ten uses, and that the trench struts have been assumed to be in use for two weeks.

4.5 DISPOSAL OF WATER (D25 – D26)

Keeping the surface of the site and the excavation free from surface water (D25) may require the provision of 'cut-off' drains on a hillside and then perhaps sumps and pumping.

Where excavation is to be carried out below the ground water level (water table) the item for keeping the excavation free of ground water (D26) requires examination in great detail, since extensive de-watering provision may be required. In this event a scheme should be prepared by a competent engineer giving sufficient detail so that the necessary de-watering plant may be measured and hire rates obtained. This information together with the duration obtained from the programme will enable the item to be priced accurately.

4.6 DISPOSAL OF EXCAVATED MATERIAL (D27–D32)

Material arising from the excavation work is either measured as being disposed on site or off site. In the first case the distance to be moved will be given, while if disposed off site it is usually the contractor who has to find a suitable tip.

The material to be disposed of may arise from a number of different excavating operations. Since part of the cost of disposal is taken up with the cost of the dumpers or trucks being loaded, and this depends on the speed of excavation, it can become an involved calculation. In the example given in Table 4.9 the material to be taken off site is assumed to arise from one source.

4.6.1 Removing surplus excavated material from site

A calculation for the removal of surplus material from a site is set out below as an example.

Information:
Tip located 6 km from contract;
Access good at site and tip;
Charge at tip £1.20 per load;
Excavated material: stiff clay;
Excavation arises from reduced level excavations by a 0.50m^3 hydraulic excavator with an output of 10m^3 per hour.

Selection of vehicle:
Size related to excavator, quantity of excavated material and availability. Six cubic metre tipper suitable in this case at a hire rate of £9.80 per hour including fuel and driver.

Number of trucks required:

Truck capacity allowing for bulking $\dfrac{100 \times 6}{133.33} = 4.50\,\text{m}^3$.

Cycle time:	(Mins)
Load 4.50 m³ @ 10 m³/hr	27.0
Travel to tip 6 km @ 25 km/hr	14.4
Tip (suitable allowance)	5.0
Return to site	14.4
Margin for contingencies (Approximately 10%)	6.0
	66.8

Cycles per hour: $\therefore \dfrac{60}{66.8}$ $= 0.90$

Quantity/truck/hour: $\therefore\ 0.90 \times 4.50$ $= 4.05\text{m}^3$

$$\frac{10\,\text{m}^3 \text{ of material excavated per hour}}{4.05\,\text{m}^3 \text{ per truck per hour}} = 2.469$$

Therefore three trucks are required to maintain output of excavator.

Table 4.9 Unit rate calculation for removing surplus excavated material from site

Item		Rate	Extension	Total
			(£/hr)	
4.9	Three 6m³ tipping trucks	9.80	29.40	
			(£/m³)	
	Divide by material transported per hour	10m³	2.940	
	Plus tipping charge 1.20 ÷ 4.5 m³		0.267	(£/m³)
			3.207	3.21

4.7 FILLING (D33–D39)

Generally filling is measured in cubic metres, with the exception of depths not exceeding 250 mm thick which are given in square metres. However, it is convenient to price all thicknesses initially in cubic metres (taking due account of any additional costs due to their layers), and then derive the unit rate per square metre. Since filling is measured as being equal to the void to be filled, allowance must be made in the calculations for the effect of compaction and waste.

Tables 4.10 and 4.11 set out, respectively, the material data and output standards for filling. Table 4.12 shows a unit rate calculation for filling.

Table 4.10 Material data

Materials	(kg/m^3)	Compaction and waste ($\star$%)	Delivered price (per tonne)†
Brick hardcore	1500	25	
Broken stone	2000	20	
Gravels, crushed limestone	1700	20	
Ash and clinker	700	40	
Pulverised fuel ash	1250	30	

$\star$Waste % included 5%; adjust if necessary.
†Space has been left in this column for current prices to be inserted.
Additional allowance for penetration in soft ground, particularly important with thin beds.

Table 4.11 Output standards

By hand	(hrs/m^3)
Load barrow, wheel a distance not exceeding 25 metres.	
Deposit and compact in 150 mm layers	2.50
Deposit and compact in 100 mm layers	3.00
	(hrs/m^2)
Extra for blinding top surface including wheeling a distance not exceeding 25 metres	0.50
Extra for hand packing to form vertical face	0.50
Mechanical plant	$(m^2/hr\star)$
Compact Wacker rammer	50
400 kg hand guided vibratory roller	80
Ten tonne self propelled roller	200
Spread and level hardcore filling to make up levels	(m^3/hr)
Drott B100	15
Spread and level hardcore filling to foundations Drott B100	7

$\star$Based on a total of four passes. The number of passes being dependent on the degree of compaction required and the type of material.

Table 4.12 Unit rate calculation for filling

Item		Rate	Extension	Total
4.10 *Hardcore:*				
Filling in, making up levels over 250 mm thick, depositing and compacting in layers. Note: The material can be tipped 20 m from the fill area. The ground is firm and level. Layers to be 150 mm maximum. Quantity small. .˙. wheeled by hand.				
Materials		(£/t)	(£/m³)	
1m³ Hardcore 1500 kg		6.00	9.00	
Compaction and waste		25%	2.25	
			11.25	
Plant				
$\frac{150}{1000} \times 80\text{m}^2/\text{hr}$		(£/hr)		
$= 12\text{m}^3/\text{hr}$.˙. adequate 400 kg hand guided vibratory roller £25/week (including fuel) ÷ 30 hrs/week working ÷ estimated output 2m³/hr		0.83	0.42	
Labour 150 mm layers 2½ MH/m³ Load, wheel, place, compact.		(£/GH)		
Use gang of 5 men .˙.	2m³/hr			
1 Ganger	3.90 + 0.25	4.15		
1 Vibrating roller operator	3.90 + 0.10	4.00		
3 Wheel and spread	3.90	11.70		(£/m³)
—				
5	2m³/hr	19.85	9.92	21.59

The calculation in Table 4.12 has taken into account the fact that usually plant, such as vibratory rollers, are standing idle for a high proportion of the time.

Fuel costs are usually charged separately, and no account has been taken of the possible extra cost of part loads of hardcore.

SELF-ASSESSMENT QUESTIONS

Calculate nett unit rates for the following items using current costs for materials, plant and labour.

1. Excavate trench to receive foundations; starting from reduced level maximum depth not exceeding 1.00 m.

   Information: subsoil loose material
   (a) method A: by hand   (£?/m^3);
   (b) method B: by machine   (£?/m^3).

2. Earthwork support maximum depth not exceeding 1.00 m; distance between opposing faces not exceeding 2.00 m. (£?/m^2).

   Information: Ground conditions loose material; support to consist of 50 × 200 close boarding, 75 × 100 walings in two rows and adjustable trench struts at 2.00 m centres along wales (assume that the trench is 1.00 m deep).

3. As last item but based upon an alternative method of battering the sides of the trench at the angle of repose (45°). (£?/m^2)

   Base on the use of a suitable excavator.

4. Hardcore filling in making up levels average 200 mm thick; depositing and compacting in layers (600m^2) (£?/m^2)

   Information: The material can be tipped adjacent to the fill area. A Drott type machine may be used to spread and level with a vibratory roller to compact the material.

5

CONCRETE WORK

CHAPTER OBJECTIVES

After studying this chapter you should be able to:

- appreciate the main factors that affect the cost of concrete work;

- perform calculations using representative examples.

5.1 CLASSIFICATION

The classification of concrete work in the Standard Method of Measurement of Building Works (SMM) can be seen to cover a wide variety of work, such as:

- in-situ concrete;
- reinforcement;
- formwork;
- precast concrete;
- composite construction.

Concrete work often forms the largest single item of work for a main contractor, on construction other than traditional housing, and thus merits the closest attention if the most economic methods are to be selected. In practice several different methods may be considered. They thus need pricing, before a decision can be made as to which is the most economical.

5.2 IN-SITU CONCRETE

5.2.1 Work operations

Concreting involves a chain of events—mixing, transporting, placing—and all these are inter-related so that the speed of the slowest operation governs the rest. Since the demand for concrete is often intermittent, it is important to determine the maximum output required and the total concreting period. A detailed programme is thus necessary. This programme will give the size of mixer, or mixers, and the time required on site.

The cost of the mixer and ancilliary equipment can then be calculated, and allocated in either the project overheads or in the item in the bill of quantities for 'maintaining on site all plant required for concreting'.

Mixing concrete

Table 5.1 gives the maximum outputs for concrete mixers and gang sizes.

Transporting concrete

Concrete may require to be transported horizontally, or vertically and horizontally, and any machine used for this purpose should, if possible, be capable of handling the mixer discharge in one load. Many

Table 5.1 Maximum outputs of concrete mixers and gang sizes

Size (litres)	Batches (per hr)	Output (m³/hr)	Distribution	Labour (mix)	Wheel (n.e. 30 m)
100	10	1.00	wheelbarrow	3	included
200	$\begin{cases}12 \\ 15\end{cases}$	2.40	wheelbarrow	2	3
		3.00	$\begin{cases}$dumper, \\ crane, etc.$\end{cases}$	2	dumper, crane, etc.
280	15	4.25	dumper, crane, etc.	2	dumper, crane, etc.
340	15	5.10	dumper, crane, etc.	2	dumper, crane, etc.

Note for Table 5.1
1. The 100 litre mixer is one of the smallest concrete mixers in general use, and is of the tilting drum type. A gang of three men can load and operate the mixer, and transport the concrete in wheelbarrows a distance not exceeding. (n.e.) 30 metres to give an output of 1 m³ per hour.
2. The larger mixers are usually of the reversing drum type with drag-line feed and weigh hopper, and can be operated by two men. The time taken to raise the hopper, discharge the contents into the drum, add the water and mix, then empty in one continuous discharge is about three minutes. This would give 20 batches of concrete per hour. This output is not usually achieved due to transporting methods being unable to keep up to the output of the mixer, or as a result of the placing gang restricting output and the necessity for relaxation (rest) periods.

    A more realistic cycle time would be four minutes giving 15 batches per hour.
3. If wheelbarrows are used handling 0.03 m³ without spillage, the discharge time is extended and the number of batches is reduced to 10 or 12 per hour.

machines are in use for transporting concrete, and examples of the most usual are given below, although this is not an exclusive list:

- Wheelbarrows are suitable for small quantities only, or in situations where it is impracticable to use mechanical means.
- Dumpers in the smaller range, 500 to 750 kg, are capable of carrying 0.20 m³ of concrete, and are suitable for housing sites or other situations where the concrete has to be transported over fair distances on site.
- Platform hoists, where one or two wheelbarrows are placed on a platform, are used when relatively small quantities of concrete require to be transported vertically.
- Skip hoists are suitable for larger quantities and where high production rates are required.
- Cranes of many types are now in use, such as truck cranes, crawler cranes and tower cranes. These cranes range in lifting capacity, lift height and radius to suit most circumstances. The type chosen depends on many factors, such as the total quantities, maximum and minimum pour requirements, distance to be moved horizontally and vertically. The skip should be capable of carrying a complete batch of concrete.
- Concrete pumps are now in increasing use, either in static or mobile form, and are capable of very large outputs, e.g. 45 m³ per hour. The concrete must be specially designed for concrete pouring. This usually requires a higher cement content, and the material cost may therefore increase.

Placing concrete

Placing concrete in foundations, i.e. shovelling it into position and then levelling it, will take about one man hour per cubic metre. Concrete in other locations and categories will usually take longer to place due to restrictions in placing, etc.

Calculating the labour cost of work in foundations

With reference to Table 5.1:

100 litre mixer requires three men to mix and transport (by wheelbarrow) 1 m³ of concrete a distance not exceeding 30 m   =   3 MH/m³
In addition, labour is required to spread
and level the concrete and in plain concrete
foundations, as stated above, the usual output would be   1 MH/m³

This gives a total of   4 MH/m³

Four man hours multiplied by the appropriate all-in labour rate will then give the estimated labour cost of mixing, transporting and placing concrete in foundations. Note that in Table 5.2 between 4.25 and 4.75 man hours have been allowed per cubic metre of concrete, depending on the depth of the foundation. This suggests that the assumptions made above are somewhat optimistic.

Table 5.2 Output standards 1

Method: 100 litre mixer and wheelbarrows; distance to be wheeled not exceeding 30 m; platform hoist.

Description			Man hours (per m^3)
Plain concrete			
Foundations		100–150 mm	4.75
		150–300 mm	4.50
	exceeding	300 mm	4.25
Beds	not exceeding	100 mm	6.25
		100–150 mm	6.00
		150–300 mm	5.50
	exceeding	300 mm	5.00
Reinforced concrete			
Beds	not exceeding	100 mm	6.75
		100–150 mm	6.50
		150–300 mm	6.00
	exceeding	300 mm	5.50
Suspended slabs	not exceeding	100 mm	8.75
		100–150 mm	8.50
		150–300 mm	8.00
	exceeding	300 mm	7.50
Walls	not exceeding	100 mm	9.50
		100–150 mm	8.75
		150–300 mm	8.00
	exceeding	300 mm	7.50
Isolated beams	not exceeding	0.03 m^2	15.00
		0.03–0.10 m^2	13.00
		0.10–0.25 m^2	11.00
	excceding	0.25 m^2	10.00
Isolated columns	not exceeding	0.03 m^2	16.00
		0.03–0.10 m^2	14.00
		0.10–0.25 m^2	12.00
	exceeding	0.25 m^2	11.00

5.2.2 In-situ concrete—output standards

Tables 5.2 to 5.4 present output standards for various methods of mixing and transporting concrete.

Tables 5.5 and 5.6 give output standards for labours on concrete and sundries, respectively.

5.2.3 All-in labour rates

Operatives engaged in mixing, transporting and placing concrete are classified as labourers, but extra payments (plus rates) are paid in accordance with the National Working Rules for continuous extra skill or responsibility. The plus rates in the examples given in Table 5.7 have been adjusted to allow for the effect of National Insurance charges and any other necessary additions in the calculations of the all-in labour rate.

Table 5.3 Output standards 2

Method: 280 litre mixer and dumper, distance to be transported not exceeding 250 m.

Description			Man hours (per m³)
Plain concrete			
Foundations		100–150 mm	2.50
		150–300 mm	2.25
	exceeding	300 mm	2.00
Beds	not exceeding	100 mm	3.75
		100–150 mm	3.50
		150–300 mm	3.00
	exceeding	300 mm	2.75
Reinforced concrete			
Foundations		150–300 mm	2.50
	exceeding	300 mm	2.25
Beds	not exceeding	100 mm	4.25
		100–150 mm	4.00
		150–300 mm	3.50
	exceeding	300 mm	3.25

Table 5.4 Output standards 3

Method: 280 litre mixer; crane with concrete skip; poker vibrator.

Description			Man hours (per m^3)
Reinforced concrete superstructure			
Suspended slabs	not exceeding	100 mm	3.75
		100–150 mm	3.50
		150–300 mm	3.00
	exceeding	300 mm	2.50
Walls	not exceeding	100 mm	4.50
		100–150 mm	3.75
		150–300 mm	3.00
	exceeding	300 mm	2.50
Isolated beams	not exceeding	0.03 m^2	10.00
		0.03–0.10 m^2	8.00
		0.10–0.25 m^2	6.00
	exceeding	0.25 m^2	5.00
Isolated columns	not exceeding	0.03 m^2	11.00
		0.03–0.10 m^2	9.00
		0.10–0.25 m^2	7.00
	exceeding	0.25 m^2	6.00

Note: The crane driver and banksman are not included in the above man hours.

Table 5.5 Output standards 4

Labours on concrete	Unit	Man hours
Grading surface to cross falls	m^2	0.50
Grading surface to falls and currents	m^2	0.75
Wood float finish	m^2	0.25
Steel float finish	m^2	0.30
Power float finish	m^2	0.15

Table 5.6 Output standards 5

Sundries	Unit	Man hours
Building paper or polythene; horizontal on slabs	m²	0.05
Cold bitumen solution; two coats; horizontal on slabs	m²	0.10
Steel anchor slots cast into concrete	m	0.20
Drill mortice in concrete for expansion bolt:		
8 mm diameter × 100 mm depth	No.	0.20
16 mm diameter × 150 mm depth	No.	0.30
Form hole through unset concrete:		
50 mm diameter × 150 mm depth	No.	0.40
100 mm diameter × 200 mm depth	No.	0.60

Table 5.7 All-in rates for operatives engaged in concrete production

	Plus rate (£)	All-in rate (£)
Labourer wheeling concrete		3.90
Concrete mixer operator:		
up to 200 litre capacity	0.10	4.00
over 200 litre, but not including 400 litre	0.20	4.10
Mechanical drag shovel operator	0.15	4.05
Dumper driver up to 2000 kg capacity	0.15	4.05
Concrete leveller or vibrator operator	0.15	4.05
Platform hoist operator	0.20	4.10
Ganger (rate varies, but not less than		
highest paid member of gang)	0.25	4.15

* It has been assumed that all the men placing concrete may have to level the surface or use vibrators, and this is therefore the rate used for men placing concrete.

5.2.4 Typical gang sizes and average labour rates

The type of work and quantities involved should determine the methods to be employed and, consequently, the concreting gang composition and size, as in the following examples:

Gang A

This gang is suitable for house foundations and small works.

Method: 100 litre mixer and wheelbarrows.

		(£)
1 mixer operator/filler	4.00	4.00
2 filler/barrowmen	3.90	7.80
1 placer	4.05	4.05
4 total		15.85
Average rate/hr ÷ 4 =		3.96

Gang B

This gang is suitable for reinforced concrete foundations and beds on larger contracts.

Method: 280 litre mixer and dumper.

		(£)
1 ganger	4.15	4.15
1 mixer operator	4.10	4.10
1 filler (drag line feed operator)	4.05	4.05
1 dumper driver	4.05	4.05
3 placers	4.05	12.15
7		28.50
Average rate/hr ÷ 7 =		4.07

Gang C

This gang is suitable for reinforced concrete structures.

Method: 280 litre mixer; crane with concreteskip; poker vibrator.

		(£)
1 ganger	4.15	4.15
1 mixer operator	4.10	4.10
1 filler	4.05	4.05
3 placers	4.05	12.15
6	——	24.45
Average rate/hr ÷ 6 =		4.08

Gang D

This gang is suitable for reinforced concrete superstructures.

Method: Pre-mixed concrete; crane with concrete skip; poker vibrator.

			(£)
1 ganger		4.15	4.15
3 placers		4.05	12.15
4			16.30
Average rate/her	÷ 4 =		4.08

Note

Gangs C and D, where a crane is utilised, will also require a banksman to fill the concrete skip and signal the crane driver.

The cost of the banksman may be allowed for when pricing the crane, and has therefore not been included in the above calculations.

5.2.5 Material costs

The following information is now required in order to calculate the cost per cubic metre of concrete: the specified mix; the prices of cement and aggregates; and the relative weights of the materials.

Concrete mixes

There are three methods in use for specifying concrete mixes:

1. Specification by volume, e.g. 1:2:4 mix being one part cement, two parts fine aggregate and four parts course aggregate by volume. This method has been widely used in the past and is widely understood, but has been superceded to a great extent by the following two specification methods.
2. Specification by weight—called 'prescribed mixes'. The most common method now in use being as defined in CP 110: part 1:1972 and BS 5328: 1976. (See Table 5.8 which has been derived from CP 110, Table 50.)
3. Specification by performance—called 'designed' mixes. The specifications may call for concrete of a certain minimum strength, e.g. 31.5 N/mm^2, with a minimum specified cement content to ensure durability.

Material prices

Table 5.9 gives material prices for Portland cement, delivered on site, and for a range of aggregates. A column has been left blank for you to enter current prices.

Table 5.8 Prescribed mixes for ordinary structural concrete

Grade of concrete	Cement (kg)	Fine aggregate (kg)	Course aggregate (kg)
C10P	240	620	1230
C15P	280	600	1200
C20P	320	600	1200
C25P	360	580	1170
C30P	400	570	1130

Note
The proportions given in Table 5.8 will normally provide concrete of the strength in N/mm^2 indicated by the grade.

The percentage of fine aggregate to total aggregate has been taken as approximately 33⅓%. The actual percentage depends on the grading zones of the fine aggregates.

Table 5.9 Material prices (delivered to site)

	Current prices (£/tonne)
Ordinary Portland cement (OPC)	
Deliveries: 15 tonne loads	55.18
10 tonne loads	55.58
7.50 tonne loads	62.90
5 tonne loads	68.80
2.50 tonne loads	75.95
1 tonne load	81.20
The above prices are for cement delivered, including non-returnable paper bags (50 kg bags). Where cement is delivered in pressurized vehicles the prices are:	
15 tonne loads	48.10
10 tonne loads	48.50
Aggregates all to BS 882	
Fine aggregate	
Course aggregate 20 mm	
Course aggregate 40 mm	

Note that the price of cement is very dependent on the quantity delivered. Thus, for small jobs, such as repairs, the price of concrete work on the basis of the material cost alone will be significantly greater than for larger jobs.

Cement price used based on 10 tonne loads in bags (£/tonne):	51.58
Add for unloading 0.50 hrs @ 3.90 (£/tonne):	1.95
Total	53.53

Since there is a limited number of concrete mixes compared to the large number of concrete measured items, it is convenient to calculate the material cost separately for each classification.

Tables 5.11 and 5.12 show two methods of calculating the material cost.

5.2.5 Ready-mixed concrete (pre-mixed concrete)

More than half the total amount of in-situ concrete placed by contractors is now supplied by the ready-mixed concrete industry. So it

Table 5.10 Material weights

Material weights	(kg/m³)
Portland cement	1440
Fine aggregate	1700
Course aggregate	1600

1:3:6 mix (11.50 N/mm²); 40 mm aggregate.

Table 5.11 Material cost for volume specification
1:3:6 mix (11.50 N/mm²); 40 mm aggregate.

(m³)			(t)	(£/t)	(£)
1 Ordinary Portland cement (OPC)	@ 1440 kg		1.44	53.53	77.08
3 Fine aggregate	@ 1700 kg		5.10	5.75	29.33
6 Course aggregate	@ 1600 kg		9.60	5.90	56.64
					163.05
Add for voids				50%	81.53
					244.58
Waste in stock pile and in place				5%	12.23
10 Divide by total m³				10	256.81
Material cost				(£/m³)	25.68

Table 5.12 Material cost for prescribed mixes

Mix prefix		A		B		C		D	
Strength (N/mm²)		C30P		C20P		C15P			
Materials	Price	Quan-tity	(£)	Quan-tity	(£)	Quan-tity	(£)	Quan-tity	(£)
	(£/t)	(kg)		(kg)		(kg)		(kg)	
OPC	48.50	400	19.40	320	15.52	280	13.58		
Fine aggregate	5.75	570	3.28	600	3.45	600	3.45		
Course aggregate	5.90	1130	6.67	1200	7.08	1200	7.08		
			29.35		26.05		24.11		
Waste		5%	1.47		1.30		1.21		
Material cost (£/m³)			30.82		27.35		25.32		

The price of cement has been based on 10 tonne loads delivered in pressurized vehicles to a site.

is usual to consider the supply of ready-mixed concrete for most contracts. Ready-mixed concrete can be supplied by truck mixers in one of several ways:

- the concrete is mixed at the depot and is agitated during transit;
- the concrete is mixed during transit, the material being dry batched and water added at the depot;
- the concrete is mixed at the site, the material being dry batched at the depot and water added on arrival at the site.

The last method is necessary when travelling from the depot to the site will take a considerable time.

Possible advantages

An area of say 10m × 10m will be required for siting the mixing plant and aggregate storage; this area may not be available on a city site. The quality of concrete will be better than average. The British Ready Mixed Concrete Association lays down minimum standards, and many depots hold quality control certificates. In many instances concrete may only be required intermittently, say one day in three. Thus the mixing plant will stand idle on site, yet will still cost money to hire. The concrete mixing gang may be employed on other work, but difficulty might be experienced in keeping them fully occupied. Very large quantities of ready-mixed concrete can be supplied in one day, e.g. the concrete required for the base to an 18 storey block of flats amounting to 640 m³ was supplied by 24 ready-mix trucks on a shuttle service between 5.30 am and 2 pm.

$$\frac{640 \ m^3}{8\frac{1}{2} \ hrs} \ = \ 75 \ m^3/hour$$

London Hilton Hotel offers another example:
30 600 m³ supplied in 56 weeks   = 546 m³/week;
largest single pour 917 m³ in 11½ hrs   =   80 m³/hr.

Points to watch

The usual load is 5 m³—smaller loads incur a surcharge.

Extra cost can be incurred due to waiting and excess time in off-loading; anything over 30 minutes on site carries an extra charge in most instances.

Good strong access is required on site for the very heavy trucks.

Careful timing of deliveries is required, since the supply company has no liability for losses arising out of delay. Sufficient labour must be available to distribute and place concrete quickly before initial set. Waste should be less than when mixing on site, since stockpile waste is not incurred. However, waste will arise during transporting and placing operations on site; a 2% allowance is suggested, but this may vary according to circumstances.

Cost comparison with mix on site

Convenience may be a factor in the decision to use ready-mixed concrete, but price is of course usually paramount.

A price comparison should be based on the whole process of mixing, transporting and placing the concrete. Furthermore, the comparison should take into account the influence on other dependent operations such as formwork and reinforcement, and most importantly the construction programme. It is usually not sufficient to consider just the relative unit rates per cubic metre, since the project overhead costs may be altered considerably.

5.2.6 Additional costs

It is necessary to study the specification and placing requirements carefully to allow for the cost of construction joints in beds, suspended slabs and walls. Where these joints are required for expansion or contraction purposes, they will be measured under clause F7 of the SMM. They can be very expensive to form, particularly, if as is usual, the reinforcement is continuous necessitating complicated 'spilt' formwork. Where the joints occur due to the contractor's method of placing—usually because the end of a day's work has been reached—these joints will have to be measured by the estimator, priced as usual and added to the cost of the relevant concrete items. Curing concrete slabs will be priced on a superficial basis.

5.2.7 Examples of typical unit rate calculations for in-situ concrete

In order to give examples of 'typical' unit rate calculations, the following examples (Tables 5.13–5.14) are only exceptionally related to the hypothetical project, e.g. item 5.2.

Table 5.13 Unit rate calculation for plain in-situ concrete 1:3:6 mix 40 mm aggregate

Item	Rate	Extension	Total
		$(£/m^3)$	
5.1 *Foundations in trenches 150–300 mm thick (F. 6.2)*			
Method: 100 litre mixer and wheelbarrows; distance to be wheeled not exceeding 30 m.			
Materials			
1:3:6 mix as perviously calculated		25.68	
Labour			
4.5 MH based upon use of gang A average rate	3.96	17.82	43.50

The above example is for the foundation to a house and where the mix is specified on a volume basis.

Table 5.14 Unit rate calculation for reinforced in-situ concrete C20P

Item	Rate	Extension	Total
5.2 *Beds 100–150mm thick (F. 6.8)*		$(£/m^3)$	
Method: 280 litre mixer, dumper and vibrating screed; distance to be conveyed not exceeding 250 m.		$(£/m^3)$	
Materials			
C20P mix as previously calculated		27.35	
Labour			
3.5 MH based upon use of gang B average rate	4.07	14.24	41.59

This example is for a large contract, say, the three-storey office block of our hypothetical project, having sufficient concrete to justify using a dumper.

Table 5.15 Unit rate calculation for reinforced in-situ concrete C30P

Item	Rate	Extension	Total
5.3 *Isolated column 0.03–0.10 m² (F. 6.15)*		($/m³)	
Method: 280 litre mixer; crane with concrete skip; poker vibrator.			
Materials			
C30P mix as previously calculated		30.82	
Labour			
9 MH based upon use of gang C average rate	4.08	36.72	67.54

Since the work set out in Table 5.15 is part of a multistorey office, it has been decided to employ a crane to transport the concrete both horizontally and vertically.

Table 5.16 Unit rate calculation for use of ready-mixed concrete

Item	Rate	Extension	Total
5.4 *Suspended slabs 150–300 mm thick (F.6.9)*		($/m³)	
Method: Ready mix; crane with concrete skip; poker vibrator			
Materials			
C30P delivered (ready mix concrete)		35.27	
Waste	3%	1.06	
		36.33	
Labour			
Based upon the use of gang D: 4 men in total. Consulting output standards (Table 5.4) the man hours are given as 3. However, this is based on mixing on site using a gang of 6 men. Therefore, the appropriate time allowance would be 2 MH.			
4/6 × 3 = 2MH	4.08	8.16	44.49

Table 5.17 Unit rate calculation for labours on concrete

Item	Rate	Extension	Total
5.5 *Travelling surfaces*			($/m²)
(hrs)			
0.30 Craftsmen	4.60		1.38

The preceding example (Table 5.16) is based on the use of ready-mixed concrete.

5.3 REINFORCEMENT

5.3.1 Bar reinforcement

Material costs

Bar reinforcement is bought by the tonne, on the basis of 25 mm bars and upwards in long stock lengths in minimum 15 tonne loads. Additional charges are made for smaller diameter bars, shorter lengths, and smaller loads. It may be delivered to site in random lengths, or cut, bent, tagged and bundled in accordance with the bar bending schedules. The standard length is 12 metres. Due to rolling margin (tolerance on rollers) bars may be slightly overweight when compared with the measured quantity—allow an addition of 1% to cover this additional cost. Careful account should be taken of the type of steel used, e.g. mild steel to BS 4449, or high tensile steel to BS 4461.

Labour costs

Allow for off-loading and stacking, including sorting on delivery, and checking with schedule, three man hours per tonne. Descaling should be allowed for if the steel is to be on site for any length of time. In addition, allow 5 hrs/tonne for transporting the steel, after it has been cut and bent, to the steel fixer. Steel fixers may be used for all the operations above, or a gang, including labourers, may be employed. Reinforcement in columns, beams and walls may need an extra 25% on the above hours. Similarly, reinforcement in stirrups, links and the like, may need an extra 50%.

Table 5.18 Output standards for bars in floors

Size (mm)	Man hours per tonne			
	Cut to length	*Bend*	*Fix*	*Total*
10	7	26	40	73
12	6	22	35	63
16	5	20	30	55
20	4	19	27	50
25	3	17	25	45

Binding wire is not included in the quantities measured, and an allowance varying between 10 and 20 kg per tonne should be made for this, i.e. 1 to 2% by weight. Additional allowances should be made for fixing accessories as required (spacers, etc.). An addition of 1% is suggested. The following allowances should be made for waste: cut and bent on site allow 5%; supplied cut and bent allow 2½%.

Allow in the project overheads for the cost of:

● Stacking area—say level ground and spread and level hardcore later removed;
● Protection (tarpaulines, shelter, to keep off rain if on site a long time);
● Bending tables and machines, cutting machines and necessary shelters.

Qualified benders and fixers of bars for reinforced concrete work are paid craftsmen's rate. Simple bar-bending or fixing may however be carried out by labourers at the labourers' rate.

Table 5.19 Unit rate calculation for bar reinforcement

Item		Rate	Extension	Total
5.6	*Bar reinforcement to BS 4449 (mild steel)*: including bends, hooks, tying wire and spacers; in foundations; 16mm diameter.			
	Materials		(£/t)	
	16mm bars delivered in random lengths		308.00	
	Rolling margin	1%	3.08	
			311.08	
	Waste	5%	15.55	
			326.63	
	Fixing accessories	1%	3.27	
10kg	Tying wire	55p	5.50	335.40
Labour				
3MH	Unload, sort and check	4.60	13.80	
55MH	Cut, bend and fix	4.60	253.00	
5MH	Transport on site	3.90	19.50	286.30
				621.70

Note:
Steelfixers have been priced in Table 5.19 for the first two items, while labourers have been used for transporting the steel on site. Alternatively, a suitable gang cost could be calculated and an average rate per man hour applied to the above output standards.

5.3.2 Welded steel fabric reinforcement

This material is supplied in sheets 4.8 m long × 2.4 m wide, or in rolls. Care must be taken in calculating the correct allowance for laps, as required in the specification. If the laps required are 150 mm, then the allowance will amount to 10%. In addition an allowance of 5% should be made for cutting waste. The output standards shown in Tables 5.20 and 5.21 are intended to apply to large areas of reinforcement. Smaller jobs may require an addition of up to 50% to the times allowed.

Table 5.20 Output standards for welded steel fabric reinforcement★

			Gang hours/m^2†				
Mesh	BS	(kg/m²)	Roads	Beds	Susp-ended floors	Walls	Columns and beams
Square	A393	6.16	0.045	0.055	0.075	0.200	
	A252	3.95	0.040	0.045	0.055		
	A193	3.02	0.035	0.040	0.050		
	A142	2.22	0.030	0.035	0.045	0.100	
	A 98	1.54	0.025	0.030	0.040		
Structural	B1131	10.90	0.070	0.080	0.105		
	B 785	8.14	0.055	0.065	0.090		
	B 503	5.93	0.045	0.055	0.075		
	B 385	4.53	0.040	0.050	0.060		
	B 283	3.73	0.040	0.045	0.055		
	B 196	3.05	0.035	0.040	0.050		
Long mesh	C 785	6.72	0.050	0.060	0.080		
	C 636	5.55	0.045	0.055	0.070		
	C 503	4.34	0.040	0.050	0.060		
	C 385	3.41	0.040	0.045	0.055		
	C 283	2.61	0.030	0.035	0.045		
Wrapping	D 49	0.77	—	—	—	—	0.080
fabric	D 31	0.49	—	—	—	—	0.050

Gang cost:
		(£)
1 steel fixer	@	4.60
1 labourer	@	3.90
		8.50 per hour

★ Welded steel fabric to BS 4483 (flat sheets, 4.8 × 2.4 m).
† Including unloading, stacking, handling, straight cutting and fixing. The cost of transportation on large sites and/or any craneage has to be considered separately and priced in the project overheads.

Table 5.21 Unit rate calculation for fabric reinforcement

Item		Rate	Extension	Total
5.7	*Fabric reinforcement:* BS 4483; 150 mm side laps, 300 mm end laps; ground slabs; A 142.		($/m^2$)	
	Materials 1 m² Fabric reinforcement A 142;			
	2.22 kg/m²		0.770	
	Laps	10%	0.077	
			0.847	
	Waste	5%	0.042	
	Spacers	say	0.050	
			0.939	
	Labour 0.035GH Unloading, stacking,			
	handling,	8.50	0.297	($/m^2$)
	straight cutting and fixing		1.236	

5.4 FORMWORK

Formwork may be classified into two basic types:

1. *Traditional formwork* is a combination of softwood framing with softwood or plywood facing and metal struts or supports. The necessary materials are usually purchased for each site with the supports being hired. Therefore the cost is partly based on the quantity of materials to be purchased and partly on the number of supports and the time they are to be hired.

Table 5.22 Striking times for formwork (days) (using Ordinary Portland Cement)

Forms and supports	3° to 15°C	15°C
All vertical forms	6	1
Slab soffits struck and repropped	10	3
Beam soffits struck and repropped	14	7
Props under slabs removed	21	10
Props under beams removed	35	16

2. *System formwork* is a combination of metal framed panels and metal struts, or supports of a proprietary nature.

System forms may be purchased or hired, but as the components are invariably looked on as items of non-mechanical plant (like scaffolding) the charge to the site is on a quantity and time basis.

Table 5.22 sets out the striking times for different types of formwork under varying temperature conditions. These times will help in the preparation of a programme to determine either the number of uses or the time that the formwork is required.

5.4.1 Material prices for formwork

The following prices have been used in calculating the formwork rates. Space has been left for you to insert the current figures if you wish.

		($£/m^3$)	($£/m^3$)
Softwood delivered to site		227.85	
Unload 0.5 hr	3.90	1.95	
		229.80	
		($£/m^2$)	($£/m^2$)
Formply 18 mm		8.35	
Unload 0.01 hr	3.90	0.04	
		8.39	
		($£$)	($£$)
Nails (0.25 kg/m^2) kg		0.60	
Mould oil (0.051/m^2) litre		0.40	
Hire rates			
		($£$/week)	($£$/week)
Telescopic steel props			
1.75–3.12 m		0.24	
2.44–3.96 m		0.27	
Telescopic steel floor centres			
Span up to 4.17 m		0.54	
5.56 m		0.62	

Table 5.23 presents the output and materials standards for formwork. Referring to Table 5.23 the following points can be made:

- The quantities of timber framing should be obtained by measurement from typical formwork drawings.
- The cost of making panels should be divided by the number of uses expected from the formwork.

Prior to placing the concrete the formwork should be examined to see that it is clean, and that there is no debris lying on the surface of horizontal formwork. A compressor with air lines may be required to 'blow out' the formwork, and the cost should be assessed and added either in the item for plant or in the project overheads.

Table 5.23 Output and material standards for formwork

	Item	Timber framing excluding boarding★ (m³)	Man hours (per/m²)		
			Make	Fix	Strip
	Superficial (m²)				
1	Soffits: horizontal				
1.1	floors or the like	0.025	—	1.25	0.70
1.2	floors or the like; strutting over 3.50 m n.e. 5 m high	0.025	—	1.55	0.90
1.3	floors or the like: over 200 mm thick For every additional 100 mm thickness add	0.015	—	0.40	0.20
2	Soffits: sloping				
2.1	floors or the like	0.030	—	2.00	1.00
3	Sides: vertical				
3.1	foundations or the like	0.050	—	1.50	0.50
3.2	walls or the like	0.045	2.00	1.00	0.50
3.3	columns or the like	0.040	2.20	1.25	0.50
4	Sides: battering				
4.1	foundations or the like	0.055	—	2.00	0.50
4.2	walls or the like	0.050	2.00	1.25	0.50
5	Sides and soffits				
5.	Wall openings, recesses, projecting panels or the like	0.060	—	2.50	1.25
5.2	beams or the like: horizontal	0.050	2.20	1.50	0.80
5.3	beams or the like: horizontal isolated	0.055	2.20	2.00	0.90
	Lineal items (m)				
6	Edges				
6.1	beds, footpaths and the like 100 mm wide	0.005	—	0.12	0.05
6.2	each additional 50 mm width	0.002	—	0.05	0.02
6.3	suspended floors and the like 100 mm wide	0.006	—	0.20	0.10
6.4	each additional 50 mm width	0.003	—	0.10	0.05
7	Sides				
7.1	kerbs and upstands 100 mm wide	0.006	—	0.20	0.10
7.2	each additional 50 mm width	0.003	—	0.10	0.05

Applicable to all items in table:	Labour (hours per m²)
Transport on site	0.20
Clean and oil	0.15

Repairs:
Where formwork panels are used more than five times, an allowance for labour and materials in repairs should be made.
★ also excludes props to soffits, beams, etc.

Table 5.24 Unit rate calculation for formwork to soffits of horizontal slabs

Item			Rate	Extension	Total

5.8 *Formwork to soffits of horizontal slabs.*
Method: 19 mm formply; 44 × 100 joists (beams)
at 400 centres; 75 × 150 runners (beams)
at 1200 centres; telescopic steel props
at 1200 centres required for 3 weeks
per use. Six uses in all.
Consider an area of $20 × 5\,m = 100\,m^2$
Calculate the quantity of materials required:

(m^3)

Joists $\quad \dfrac{5.00}{0.400} = 13 + 1/20.00 × 44 × 100 \qquad 1.232$

Runners $\dfrac{2000}{1.200} = 17 + 1/5.00 × 75 × 150 \qquad \dfrac{1.013}{2.245}$

Props (under runners)
$\therefore\ 5\,m ÷ 1.2\,m = 4 + 1 = 5$ props/runner
$\qquad\qquad × 18$ runners $\qquad = \qquad 90N^r$

$(£/100\,m^2)$

Materials					
	Formply 18 mm	$100\,m^2$	8.39	839.00	
	Softwood	$2.245\,m^3$	229.80	515.90	
				1354.90	
	Initial waste		7½%	101.62	
	Divide by uses		6	1456.52	
	Cost per use		$\therefore$	242.75	
	Steel props $90N^r × 3$ weeks		0.24	64.80	
	Nails				
	$\quad (100\,m^2 × 0.25\,kg)\ 25\,kg$		0.50	12.50	
	Mould oil				
	$\quad (100\,m^2 × 0.50$ litre) 5 litre		0.40	2.00	322.05

Labour					
$(hrs/100\,m^2)$					
125	Make and fix (carpenter)		4.60	575.00	
70	Strip (labourer)		3.90	273.00	
20	Transport (labourer)		3.90	78.00	
15	Clean and oil (labourer)		3.90	58.50	984.50
					£1306.55
Rate (per m^2)			$÷ 100 =$		£13.07

Table 5.24 sets out a unit rate calculation for formwork to soffits of horizontal slabs.

Although the cost of the formwork has been based on six uses, a repair allowance has not been made. The work is straightforward, and it is anticipated that with proper oiling and cleaning the plywood will strip easily and that, with reasonable care, the timber will last for at least six uses.

Tables 5.25 and 5.26 respectively, present unit rate calculations for formwork to sides of vertical walls, and to sides of isolated columns.

Table 5.25 Unit rate calculations for formwork to sides of vertical walls

Item		Rate	Extension	Total
5.9	*Formwork to sides of vertical walls.* Method: 19 mm formply fabricated into panels with 50×100 softwood framing and wales. Five uses expected. Consider an area of $1\,m^2$ using data from past records of similar constructions.		$(£/m^2)$	$(£/m^2)$
	Materials			
$1\,m^2$	Formply 18 mm	8.39	8.39	
$0.045\,m^3$	Softwood framing and wales	229.80	10.34	
			18.73	
	Initial waste	7½%	1.40	
	Divide by uses	÷5	20.13	
	Cost per use			
	Form ties and nails		0.20	
	Mould oil		0.02	4.25
	Labour (MH/m²)			
2.00	Make into panels (Carpenters)	4.60	9.20	
	Divide by uses	÷5	1.84	
1.00	Fix (Carpenters)	4.60	4.60	
0.50	Strip (Carpenters)	4.60	2.30	
0.20	Transport (Labourers)	3.90	0.78	
0.15	Clean and oil (Labourers)	3.90	0.58	10.10
				14.35

Table 5.26 Unit rate calculations for formwork to sides of isolated columns

Item				Rate	Extension	Total
5.10	*Formwork to sides of isolated columns 300 × 500.*					
	Method: Base on hire of proprietory (system) formwork @ £3.50/m²/week.					
	The programme indicates that the formwork is in use over a period of 15 weeks including an allowance for holiday and initial assembly time: nine column forms are in use at any one time.					
	Quantity as per bill: 324 m.					
	Consider the price for the total area: 324 m × girth of 1.60 m = 518 m².					
	Drawings indicate columns 3.00 m high thus area of nine columns: 9/1.60 × 3.00 = 43.20 m².					
	Materials				(£/324 m)	
	43.20 m²	Hire panels × 15 weeks		3.50	2 268.00	
		Damage/loss		5%	113.40	
	36 N	Steel props (4 per column) × 15 weeks		0.24	129.60	
		Damage/loss		5%	6.48	
	518 m²	Mould oil		0.02	10.36	2 527.84
	Transport					
		Deliver and return 2 part loads		30.00	60.00	60.00
	Labour (MH/m²)		(m²)	(MH)		
	2.20	Initial assembly	43.20	95.04		
	1.25	Fix	518.00	647.50		
	0.50	Strip	518.00	259.00		
	2.20	Dismantle	43.20	95.04		
		Carpenters		1 096.58	4.60	5 044.27
	0.20	Transport on site	518.00	103.60		
	0.15	Clean and oil	518.00	77.70		
		Labourers		181.30	3.90	707.07	5 751.34
						8 339.18
		Rate per metre		÷ 324		£25.74
		Rate per square metre— sometimes useful for comparison purposes		÷ 518		£16.10

In the case set out in Table 5.25, carpenters have been taken on for stripping the formwork. This is because it is thought that more care will be needed (due to form ties, etc.) than for formwork to floors.

SELF-ASSESSMENT QUESTIONS

Calculate nett unit rates for the following items using current costs for materials, plant and labour.

1. Plain in-situ concrete 1:2:4 mix in beds over 100 mm not exceeding 150 mm thick. ($£?/m^3$)

   (This is the oversite concrete to a house and the distance from the mixer is 20 m).

2. Reinforced in-situ concrete C15P in foundations over 150 mm not exceeding 300 mm thick. ($£?/m^3$)

   (This work is in connection with a warehouse and the distance the concrete has to be transported from the mixer averages 100 m.)

3. 20 mm bar reinforcement to BS 4449 (mild steel) including bends, hooks, tying wire and spacers in columns. ($£?/t$)

4. Formwork to sides of vertical foundations or the like. ($£?/m^2$) (Four uses of the timber are expected.)

5. Formwork to sides and soffits of beams or the like. ($£?/m^2$) (Five uses of the panels and supporting timbers expected.)

6

BRICKWORK
AND
BLOCKWORK

┌─────────────────────────┐
│   CHAPTER OBJECTIVES   │
└─────────────────────────┘

After studying this chapter you should be able to:

- appreciate the main factors that affect the cost of brickwork and blockwork;
- calculate representative examples.

6.1 INTRODUCTION

Some of the factors that may affect the cost of brickwork and blockwork are listed below.

Weather conditions, e.g. if it is likely to rain or freeze, protection may have to be given and the work performance will decrease; the continuity or otherwise of the work (long straight walls or difficult broken-up work); repetition; location and height of walls; accessibility; type of bond; thickness of walls; type and weight of bricks and blocks; and all of these factors will affect the output of the bricklayers.

6.2 CLASSIFICATION

The 'brickwork and blockwork' section of the Standard Method of Measurement includes the following work:

- Brickwork;
- Brick facework;
- Blockwork;

- Damp-proof courses;
- Sundries.

I will now consider each of these in turn.

6.3 BRICKWORK

6.3.1 Brick sizes

The Standard brick size is $215 \times 102.5 \times 65$ mm which gives a format of $225 \times 112.5 \times 75$ with 10 mm joints.

Thus the number of bricks per square metre is: 59 per half brick wall; and 118 per one brick wall.

The weights of different types of bricks are given in Table 6.1.

Table 6.1 Weight of bricks size $225 \times 102.5 \times 65$ mm

Type of brick	(kg/brick)
Clay, common or facing	2.14–3.10
Clay engineering	3.27–4.16
Sand lime (calcium silicate)	2.72–3.40
Concrete	3.00–5.00

6.3.2 Waste

Waste on bricks can occur because of: damage during unloading, stacking and handling or by the action of frost or dirt; and rejection due to poor face or shape; or cutting to special bonds. All the above factors will be influenced by the type and quality of brick and site conditions.

Table 6.2 Typical waste percentages

Type of brick	(%)
Soft facings	10
Normal facings	7½
Fletton bricks	5
Hard commons	4
Engineering bricks	4

Due to a combination of the factors shown in Table 6.2 and poor site management, waste percentages greatly in excess of those given have been recorded.

6.3.3 Brickwork mortar

Table 6.3 sets out the material prices for mortar.

Table 6.3 Brickwork mortar

Material prices	Used in Calculations (£/t)	Current (£/t)
Ordinary Portland Cement (OPC)	76.80	
Unload labour ½ hr @ 3.90	1.95	
	78.75	
Hydrated-lime	120.55	
Unload labour ½ hr @ 3.90	1.95	
	122.50	
Building sand	8.50	

You can enter current prices in the blank column.

Material cost per cubic metre of mortar

Mix 1:3 cement: sand (mortar class (ii))			(£/m³)
OPC	0.50t	78.75	39.38
Building sand	1.65t	8.50	14.03
			53.41
Waste (in stockpile)		5%	2.67
			56.08
Mix 1:1:6 cement: lime: sand (mortar class (iii))			
OPC	0.25t	78.75	19.69
Hydrated lime	0.12t	122.50	14.70
Building sand	1.70t	8.50	14.45
			48.84
Waste		5%	2.44
			51.28

Ready-mixed mortar

Mortar may be supplied in a similar fashion to ready-mixed concrete. It is made from clean, well-graded sand and lime putty, the proportions being varied to suit any specified mix. The applicable specification is BS 4721: 1971. The most commonly used mortar is 1 cement: 1 lime: 6 sand. In terms of weight this means adding 150 kg of Portland cement to 1 tonne 1:6 ready mixed lime: sand mortar. This will produce approximately $0.55\,\text{m}^3$ of mortar.

Table 6.4 Volume of mortar per m^2 of brickwork

Wall thickness	(m^3)
Half brick	0.025
One brick	0.065
One and a half brick	0.105

The volume shown in Table 6.4 is based on the use of standard size bricks without frogs. If the thickness of the mortar joints is greater than 10 mm, or the bricks have either one or two frogs, then the quantity of mortar required will naturally increase.

An allowance of 15% for waste (after mixing) has also been made in the volumes stated.

6.3.4 Plant costs

Invariably mortar will be mixed using a small concrete mixer, and the cost should be priced in the item for maintaining on site all plant required for brickwork and blockwork. Alternatively the cost may be included in the Preliminaries. Other plant to be considered may include scaffolding, masonry saws, rough terrain fork lifts, dumpers, etc.

6.3.5 Output standards for brickwork

The following labour outputs allow for unloading the bricks adjacent to the delivery vehicle:

- Unloading and stacking common bricks 1 MH per 1000.
- Unloading and stacking facings 1½ MH per 1000.

It has then been assumed that the bricklayers labourer will pick up the bricks on a hod and convey them to the bricklayer. If the bricks have to be distributed over any distance, additional labour hours should be allowed for. Alternatively, the bricks may be unloaded by the driver of the delivery vehicle using a crane attached to the vehicle, or other mechanical means may be used to unload and transport the bricks such as a rough terrain forklift.

6.3.6 Laying 65mm common bricks

Table 6.5 Output standards for laying 65 mm common bricks

| Walls | Bricks per bricklayer hour | |
	In foundations	In superstructure
1½ brick	70	65
1 brick	65	60
½ brick	55	50

Laying facing bricks

The rate of laying facing bricks will be lower than that for common bricks because of the greater care required, and a reduction of 20% in output is suggested. The output will however depend on the exact type of facing used, as some require much greater care in handling or laying than others. This is in addition to the other factors that may have to be taken into account, such as stringent specification requirements as to verticallity of perpends and regularity of courses. In addition, an allowance for fair face and pointing should be made, as shown in Table 6.6.

Table 6.6 Allowances for fair face and pointing

Fair face and pointing	(hrs/m²)
Fair face and pointing as work proceeds	0.20
Fair face as work proceeds, and pointing later with special mortar	0.40

Modification of outputs

The outputs given in Table 6.5 are for housing work, and must be modified if necessary by the factors mentioned previously.

Work in foundations is taken to be in cement mortar. Work in superstructure is taken to be in cement lime mortar, or cement mortar with plasticizing additive.

Where work is in cement mortar without additive in superstructure, reduce outputs by approximately 5%.

For work in engineering bricks, reduce outputs by approximately 20%.

6.3.7 Gang sizes

Outputs and costs are usually related to the 'bricklayer hour', which includes the time and cost of labour attendance.

Common gang size

The following labour cost figures are for common gang size. Space has been left for current figures to be inserted.

		(£/hour)	(£/hour)
2 bricklayers	4.60		9.20
1 labourer			3.90
Cost per gang hour			13.10
Cost per bricklayer hour	÷2		6.55

A different ratio of bricklayers to labourers will be necessary according to the amount of servicing required by the bricklayers, and type and amount of mechanical aids available. For example, if a rough terrain fork lift is used, we may only need one labourer to every six bricklayers. However, the appropriate cost of the relevant plant and operator must be taken into account. This cost is usually allocated in the project overheads, since a service is rendered to several gangs and possibly other trades. Alteration work may, on the other hand, require a much higher ratio of labourers, probably 1:1 due to the far greater attendance required on the bricklayers.

6.3.8 Brick facework (G14)

Half-brick walls and one-brick walls built fair both sides, or entirely of facing bricks, are measured in square metres, stating the thickness. In other cases, facework is given in square metres as extra over the brickwork on which it occurs. Thus, pricing half-brick and one-brick walls in facings follows the same pattern as for common brickwork. However, in walls which are built partly in commons and partly in facings, the calculations are slightly more complicated as can be seen from the two contrasting examples which follow (Tables 6.7 and 6.8).

6.3.9 Brickwork (G5)

Examples are now given of unit rate calculations for brickwork using the information and calculations given above.

Table 6.7 Unit rate calculation for brickwork

Item		Rate	Extension	Total
Substructure Common bricks in cement mortar (1:3); 6.1 One Brick Wall.			($/m^2$)	($/m^2$)
Materials				
118 65 mm common bricks (£/1000)				
Delivered price	99.00			
Unload: Labourer 1 hr	3.90	102.90	12.142	
Waste	4%		0.486	
0.065 m³ Cement mortar (including waste)		56.08	3.645	
			16.273	
Labour				
65 b/hr $\dfrac{118}{65}$ = 1.815 bricklayer hours		6.55	11.888	
			28.161	28.16
Superstructure Common bricks in cement lime mortar (1:1:6); 6.2 Half Brick Wall.				
Materials				
59 65 mm common bricks a.b.		102.90	6.071	
Waste		4%	0.243	
0.025 m³ cement lime mortar (including waste)		51.28	1.282	
			7.596	
Labour				
50 b/hr $\dfrac{59}{50}$ = 1.18 bricklayer hours		6.55	7.729	
			15.325	15.32

Table 6.8 Unit rate calculation for brick facework

	Item			Rate	Extension	Total
6.3	*Sub-structure* Extra over common brick-work in cement mortar (1:3) for facing bricks PC £220.00: 1000; Flush point as work proceeds; flemish bond in walls or the like.				($£/m^2$)	($£/m^2$)
79N°	*Materials* Facings (2/3 × 118)		($£/1000$)			
	Delivered price		220.00			
	Unload Labourer 1½ hrs 3.60		5.85			
			225.85			
	Waste	7½%	16.94			
			242.79			
	Less common bricks including unloading as item 6.1 102.90					
	Waste	4% 4.12	107.02	135.77	10.726	
	Labour					
65	Commons					
13	Facings	− 20%				
52						
		(BL hrs/m²)				
79/52	Facings	1.519				
79/65	Commons	1.215				
	EO	0.304				
	Flush pointing	0.200	0.504	6.55	3.301	
					14.027	14.03

Table 6.8 (*Contd.*)

	Item		Rate	Extension	Total
6.4	*Superstructure.* Half brick wall in facing bricks PC £220.00:1000; flush pointing as work proceeds; stretcher bond			(£/m²)	(£/m²)
59 N°	*Materials* Facings Delivered price Unloading by Hyab crane on delivery vehicle	(£/1000) 220.00 + 5.00			
		225.00			
	Waste	7½%	16.87	241.87	14.270
0.025 m³	Cement lime mortar (including waste)			51.28	1.282
					15.552
50 10	*Labour* Commons—bricks/hr Facings—20%				
40					
59/40	Bricklayer hours Flush pointing	(hrs/m³) 1.475 0.200			
		1.675	6.55	10.971	
				26.523	26.52

6.4 BLOCKWORK (G26)

The general remarks concerning brickwork apply equally to block-work.

6.4.1 Block sizes

Blocks are produced in many thicknesses and face dimensions. Working on a format of 400×200, including 10 mm joints, there would be 12½ blocks per square metre. Unlike bricks, blocks are sold at a price per square metre.

Table 6.9 Volume of mortar required per m² of blockwork (in m³)

Face size		Thickness					
	50	75	100	150	200	250	
400 × 200	0.005	0.006	0.008	0.012	0.016	0.020	
450 × 200	0.004	0.006	0.008	0.012	0.015	0.019	
450 × 225	0.004	0.005	0.007	0.011	0.014	0.018	

Table 6.10 Types of block and waste factors

Dense aggregate	2½%
Foamed slag and clinker	5%
Lightweight	5%

The lighter blocks are quite fragile in the thinner sizes, and the waste will be more than that indicated unless great care is taken in unloading and handling.

BS Classification

BS 2028:1968 classifies blocks as:

- Type A—dense aggregate concrete;
- Type B—lightweight aggregate for load bearing applications;
- Type C—lightweight aggregate for non-load bearing applications.

As is to be expected, the output standards for unloading and laying dense concrete blocks are much lower than for lightweight blocks. These outputs for laying will be further reduced if there is extensive cutting to bond—say at frequent openings.

6.4.2 Output standards for blockwork

Table 6.11 Unloading and stacking blocks: labourer hours per square metre

Type		Thickness (mm)						
	50	75	100	150	200	250	300	
Lightweight	0.04	0.05	0.06	0.08	0.10	0.12	0.14	
Dense concrete	0.05	0.06	0.07	0.10	0.12	0.14	—	

Table 6.12 Laying blocks: bricklayer hours per square metre

Type	Thickness (mm)						
	50	75	100	150	200	250	300
Lightweight	0.40	0.40	0.50	0.70	0.90	1.10	1.30
Dense concrete							
hollow	—	—	0.65	0.85	1.05	1.30	—
solid	0.55	0.55	0.70	0.95	1.20	—	—

Table 6.13 Unit rate calculation for blockwork

				Work section	
	Item		Rate	Extension	Total
	Lightweight blocks; keyed both sides; in cement and lime mortar (1:1:6)				
6.5	*Walls or partitions 100 mm thick*			(£/m²)	(£/m²)
	Materials				
(1 m²)	Lightweight blocks 100 mm (450 × 225)			5.500	
0.06 hrs	Unload and stack: Labour		3.90	0.234	
				5.734	
	Waste		5%	0.287	
				6.021	
0.007 m³	Mortar (waste included)		51.28	0.359	
				6.380	
	Labour				
0.50	Bricklayer hours		6.55	3.275	
				9.655	9.65

6.4.3 Output standards for sundries
See Table 6.14

Table 6.14

Sundries	Unit	Bricklayer hours
Damp-proof courses		
horizontal not exceeding 150 mm wide	m	0.08
vertical not exceeding 150 mm wide	m	0.12
Form cavity	m^2	0.10
Closing cavity at jambs or sills	m	0.35
Bedding plates or frames in mortar not exceeding 125 mm wide	m	0.05
Bedding plates or frames in mortar not exceeding 125 mm wide and pointing one side	m	0.08
Point frame in mastic	m	0.06
Cut groove in brickwork for water bar	m	0.25
Rake out joint in brickwork for turn-in edge of flashing horizontal; and pointing	m	0.15
Rake out joint in brickwork for turn-in edge of flashing stepped and pointing	m	0.25
Building in metal windows; cutting and pinning lugs; including unloading and handling		
Not exceeding 0.50 m^2	m^2	2.50
0.50–1.00 m^2	m^2	2.00
1.00–3.00 m^2	m^2	1.75
over 3.00 m^2	m^2	1.25
Cutting chases in brickwork		
for one pipe; small; vertical	m	0.30
for one pipe; large; vertical	m	0.45
Holes for pipes or the like; small		
half brick wall	No.	0.30
one brick wall	No.	0.65
Holes for pipes or the like; large		
half brick wall	No.	0.40
one brick wall	No.	0.90

Table 6.15 Unit rate calculations for damp-proof courses and sundries

Item			Rate	Work section Extension	Total
6.6		Damp Proof Courses (DPCs) *Polythene to BS 743 horizontal damp-proof course 112.5 mm wide.*		(£/m)	(£/m)
	1m	*Materials* DPC (30 m rolls)	3.30	0.110	
		Waste and Laps	5%	0.005	
				0.115	
	0.08	*Labour* Bricklayer hours	6.55	0.524	
				0.639	0.64
6.7		Sundries *Forming 50 mm cavities in hollow walls; 3 butterfly ties per m².*		(£/m²)	(£/m²)
	3 No	*Materials* Wall ties to BS 1243 galvanized per 1000	56.80	0.170	
		Waste	10%	0.017	
				0.187	
	0.10	*Labour* Fixing ties and keeping cavity clear Bricklayer hours	6.55	0.655	
				0.842	0.84

```
┌─────────────────────────────────────────────┐
│   SELF-ASSESSMENT QUESTIONS                   │
└─────────────────────────────────────────────┘
```

Calculate nett unit rates for the following items using current costs for materials and labour.

1. Facing bricks in cement-lime mortar (1:2:9). One brick wall, fair faced both sides, flush pointed both sides as work proceeds; Flemish bond.

   Quantity 520 m² £?/m²

2. Lightweight concrete blocks in cement-lime mortar (1:2:9) 200 mm thick in partitions. Quantity 660 m² £?/m²

3. Given two gangs of bricklayers each having two bricklayers, determine how long each of the above items will take to construct and what size of mortar mixer will be required. The bricklayers are not limited to one type of work. The maximum outputs of mixers are given in the chapter on Concrete Work.

7

WOODWORK

CHAPTER OBJECTIVES

After studying this chapter you should be able to:

- appreciate the main factors that affect the cost of woodwork items;
- calculate representative examples.

7.1 CLASSIFICATION

The Standard Method of Measurement of Building Works 6 has the new Woodwork section in place of two previous classifications of Carpentry and Joinery. The section now ranges from structural framing work to sheet linings and staircases. In essence, most of the work undertaken by the Carpenter or Joiner is included in this section; exceptions are fencing, see section X, and dry linings and partitions, see section T.

7.2 INTRODUCTION

The most important factors to be considered when pricing woodwork are as follows: The preambles, or specification, should be read very carefully to ascertain the exact type and quality of material specified, e.g. the material may be referred to as hardwood in the item description in the bills, which could mean anything from keruing, one of the cheapest hardwoods, to teak, one of the most expensive, as can be seen from the index of materials cost on the following page. Note must also be taken of any reference to codes of practice, and in the case of structural timbers, to any stress grading limitations. The drawings may indicate the degree of complexity of the work, e.g. roof plans and sections would enable an assessment to be made of the framing details and difficulties that might be experienced in fabrication and erection. If softwood is planed, or machined in any way, payment is made on the nominal (sawn) size, not the finished size unless to special order.

Softwood is available in lengths beginning at 1.8 m, increasing by increments of 300 mm.

The price quoted varies according to such factors as:

grade   +7% for stress grading (GS);

length   +5% for 5.1 to 7.5 m
              +25% over 7.5 m;

cross-section—large sections may be very difficult to buy and expensive;

treatment +12½% for pressure impregnation;

quantity and distance from port of entry to site.

7.2.1 Index of materials cost

Table 7.1 gives an indication of the relative costs of various types of soft and hardwoods.

Table 7.1 Materials cost index

Material	Index
Softwood	
Carcassing quality	
up to 4.8 m lengths	100
Joinery quality	
top-grade redwood	150
Douglas fir no. 2 clear and better	250
Hardwood	
Afromosia	355
Beech	235
European oak	230
Iroko	280
Keruing	140
Meranti	200
Sapeli	275
Teak	650
West African mahogany	280

7.2.2 Standard sizes (cross-sections) of sawn softwood

Table 7.2 presents the standard sizes of sawn softwood in terms of cross-sectional areas. Space is provided for current prices to be inserted.

7.2.3 Waste allowances

Since carcassing timber is supplied in multiples of 300 mm careful

Table 7.2 Standard sizes of softwood

Thickness (mm)	Width (mm)	Cross-section (area)	Length (per m³)	Price (per m³)
19	75	1425	702	
	100	1900	526	
25	75	1875	533	
	100	2500	400	
	125	3125	320	
	150	3750	267	
32	75	2400	417	
38	75	2850	351	
44	75	3300	303	
	100	4400	227	
	125	5500	182	
	150	6600	152	
	175	7700	130	
	200	8800	114	
	225	9900	101	
	250	11000	91	
75	150	11250	89	
	175	13125	76	
	200	15000	67	
	225	16875	59	
	250	18750	53	
	300	22500	44	

Further standard sizes are available in accordance with British Standards 4471:1969.

ordering should keep cutting to length to a minimum. Suggested allowance 7½%. Lineal joinery items are also supplied in lengths of 300 mm, and would require a similar waste allowance of 7½%. Boarding and flooring requires allowance to be made for edge planing and if tongued and grooved, the allowance for the tongue. The following example illustrates how these allowances can be calculated:

	Width (mm)
Boarding nominal or basic size	150
Less 2 planed faces @ 2 mm	4
nett width if square edge	146
Less for tongue	6
	140

Addition to measured area for ordering quantity:

$$\frac{\text{reduction in width}}{\text{nett width}} \times 100$$

Therefore, in this case for tongued and grooved boarding nominal width 150 mm the percentage addition would be:

$$\frac{10}{140} \times 100 = 7.14\%$$

plus an addition for cutting waste of usually 5%.

Unframed second fixings, such as skirtings, architraves and window boards, require an allowance for cutting waste of from 5 to 10% say average 7½%.

Sheet materials often require waste allowances of 15% or more unless the design takes into account the size of sheets available—standard size, is usually 1.22 m × 2.44 m.

7.2.4 Nails

Tables 7.3–7.6 give the approximate number of nails per kilogram for the most common sizes and types. (Again, space is left for current prices to be inserted.) It should be noted that there may be a range or diameters for any particular length which will affect this figure.

7.2.5 Unloading and stacking

Allow 0.50 hrs of a labourer per m^3 for unloading and stacking carcassing timber. Other bulk items, such as floor boarding or chipboard, can be assessed on a similar basis. Alternatively, the materials may be mechanically unloaded. Unloading of lineal items such as battens, skirtings and architraves have been allowed for in the relevant output standards for fixing.

7.2.6 Transport on site

Allow for any necessary transport and double handling costs in project overheads.

Table 7.3 Bright round wire nails

Size (mm)	(No./kg)	Price (per kg)
25 × 1.80	1850	
40 × 2.36	660	
50 × 2.65	440	
65 × 3.00	280	
75 × 3.75	145	
100 × 4.50	79	
125 × 5.60	42	
150 × 6.00	31	

Table 7.4 Lost head bright round wire nails

Size (mm)	(No./kg)	Price (per kg)
50 × 3.00	375	
60 × 3.35	270	
65 × 3.35	240	
75 × 3.75	160	

Table 7.5 Bright oval wire brads

Size (mm)	(No./kg)	Price (per kg)
25	2500	
40	990	
50	495	
65	240	
75	130	
100	68	

Table 7.6 Bright annular ringed shank nails

Size (mm)	(No./kg)	Price (per kg)
25 × 2.00		
50 × 3.35		
65 × 3.35		
75 × 3.75		

7.3 GANG SIZES AND OUTPUT STANDARDS

Carpenters often work in pairs on small contracts, with occasional assistance from labourers to lift heavy items such as timber beams. On large contracts, where a lot of fetching and carrying is involved, they may work in gangs with a labourer attending and fetching timber and nails. An example of such a gang is given in Table 7.7.

Table 7.7 Carpenters' gang costs

Gang size/cost			(£/hour)
Leading carpenter	4.60+	0.25★	4.85
Carpenters	4@	4.60	18.40
Labourer	1@	3.90	3.90
Cost per gang hour			27.15
Cost per carpenter hour		÷ 5	5.43

★ Plus rates for leading carpenters vary, but not less than NWR requirement.

The gang size will be altered according to circumstances, and it may be necessary to reduce the effective time of the leading carpenter on complex work.

7.3.1 Output standards for carcassing and items in softwood

Tables 7.8–7.15 set out the output standards for carcassing items and all types of work in softwood.

Table 7.8

Carcassing items	(Man hours/m³) Sectional area (1000 mm²)		
	NE 5	EXC 5 and NE 10	EXC 10
Floors	24	21	18
Partitions	40	35	—
Flat roofs	22	20	17
Pitched roofs, including			
ceiling joists	30	26	22
Kerbs, bearers, and the like	20	18	16

Table 7.9

Carcassing items	(Man hours/m)
Herringbone strutting: 50×50mm	
to 150mm deep joists	0.35
to 250mm deep joists	0.40
Solid strutting to joists	
50×150	0.30
50×250	0.35

Table 7.10

Carcassing labours	(Man hours/item)
Notch and fit ends of timber to metal	0.25
Trim members around 1.50×0.50m opening and 50×200mm joists	2.00
Trim members around 2.50×1.00m opening and 50×250mm joists	5.00

Table 7.11

	(Man hours/m²) Widths (mm)		
First fixings—softwood	75	100	150
Board flooring: tongued and grooved joints			
19mm	0.75	0.68	0.55
22mm	0.78	0.71	0.58
25mm	0.80	0.73	0.60
Matchboarding: tongued and grooved and vee joints			
19mm: to walls internally	1.15	1.00	0.70
19mm: to ceilings	1.55	1.33	1.00
19mm: to cheeks of dormers	1.75	1.50	1.15
Roof boarding: tongued and grooved joints laid to slope			
25mm	0.68	0.62	0.50
Chipboard flooring: butt joints			
18mm		0.40	
22mm		0.42	
Chipboard flooring: tongued and grooved joints			
18mm		0.43	
22mm		0.45	

Table 7.12

First fixings—softwood	(Man hours/m)
Eaves, verge boarding, fascias and barge boards: wrought	
19 × 150	0.25
25 × 200	0.30
38 × 225	0.40
Soffit boarding: wrought	
19 × 150	0.30
19 × 300	0.50
Firrings	
50 × 50 (average) deep	0.07
50 × 75 (average) deep	0.09
Bearers	
38 ⎱ × 50 50 ⎰	0.12
Nosing: wrought	
19 ⎱ × 75 25 ⎰	0.25
Grounds and battens	
19 ⎱ × 50 25 ⎰	0.10

Table 7.13

Second fixings	(Man hours/m)
Skirtings	
19 × 75 ⎱ 19 × 100 ⎰	0.15
25 × 150	0.20
Architraves and cover fillets	
19 × 50 ⎱ 25 × 75 ⎰	0.10
Stops: screwed on	
19 × 38 ⎱ 25 × 50 ⎰	0.15
Glazing beads and the like	
13 × 19: pinned	0.10
19 × 25: fixed with cups and screws	0.20
Shelves	
22 × 150	0.30
25 × 200	0.35
Window boards	
25 ⎱ × 225 32 ⎰	0.60

Table 7.14

Composite itmes—softwood	(Man hours/each)
Doors	
External panel or flush doors 44mm thick	
up to 900mm wide	2.00
Internal flush doors 35mm thick up to	
610mm wide	1.25
over 610mm wide	1.50
Door frame and lining sets	
External door frames (per set)	1.50
Internal door linings (per set)	1.00
Casements and frames	
640 × 770	1.00
1225 × 1070	1.50
1810 × 1225	2.00
Staircases	
Standard straight flight stair	
2600 rising 2700 going 900 wide	12.00

Door frame and lining sets	(Man hours/m)
Jambs and heads	
38 × 115 to 138	0.20
64 × 89 to 115	0.25
Cills	
75 × 150 to 250	0.30
Mullions and transomes	
64 × 75	0.15

Table 7.15

Sundries	Unit	(Man hours)
Extra over fixing with nails for fixing with:		
steel screws	No.	0.08
steel screws including sinking heads		
and pellating	No.	0.25
brass screws and cups	No.	0.15
Plugging		
brickwork	No.	0.05
concrete walls	No.	0.08
concrete soffits	No.	0.10
Cartridge fired plugs		
walls	No.	0.03
soffits	No.	0.05

Table 7.15 (*Contd.*)

Sundries	Unit	(Man hours)
Holes in timber for bolts and the like		
up to 20mm diameter per 50mm depth	No.	0.10
countersink	No.	0.02
Insulating materials		
100mm insulating quilt: laid between joists	m²	0.10
100mm building roll: fixed vertically between		
timber framing	m²	0.15
building paper or vapour barrier stapled		
to joists or timber framing	m²	0.03

7.3.2 Output standards for items in hardwood

Due to the hardness of the material it takes longer to cut and bore hardwoods when compared to softwoods. Also, since the finished work will be varnished or polished, a very high standard of workmanship is required. The following multiplying factor, dependent on the type of hardwood and specification requirements, is suggested:

Oak and mahogany	1.50
Afromosia and beech	1.75
Teak and walnut	2.00

Tables 7.16 and 7.17 present output standards for metalwork and ironmongery.

Table 7.16

Metalwork	Unit	(Man hours)
Water bars including grooves in timber		
3 × 30	m	0.25
6 × 50	m	0.30
Dowels including mortice in timber		
10 × 50	No.	0.07
12 × 100	No.	0.10
Cramps		
25 × 3 × 230 mm girth; one end		
bent, holed and screwed to softwood;		
other end fishtailed for building in	No.	0.10
Straps		
32 × 2.5 mm one end screwed to		
timber, the other end built in:		

Table 7.16 (*Contd.*)

Metalwork	Unit	(Man hours)
not exceeding 600 mm girth	No.	0.25
800 to 1200 mm girth	No.	0.35
Steel joist hangers fixed to softwood		
not exceeding 150 mm deep	No.	0.10
175 to 250 mm deep	No.	0.15
Bolts and nuts		
50 to 100 mm long, not exceeding 10 mm diameter	No.	0.10
50 to 100 mm long, 12 to 20 mm diameter	No.	0.15
110 to 200 mm long, not exceeding 10 mm diameter	No.	0.12
110 to 200 mm long 12 to 20 mm diameter	No.	0.18

Table 7.17

Ironmongery	Unit	(Man hours)
Rising butts	Pair	0.25
Tee hinge	Pair	0.30
Overhead door closer	Each	2.00
Door furniture	Set	0.30
Mortice dead lock or latch	Each	1.25
Cylinder lock	Each	1.00
Postal plate	Each	1.50
Lever action flush bolt	Each	0.75
Finger plate	Each	0.20
Kicking plate	Each	0.30
Hat and coat hooks	Each	0.10
Handrail bracket	Each	0.20
Shelf bracket	Each	0.20

Notes
1. The fixing of butt hinges is included with the fixing of doors.
2. For fixing to hardwood increase the above time allowances by 33⅓%.
3. Ironmongery is usually a prime cost sum in bills of quantities and the estimator has to allow for:
   Taking delivery, storing and fixing. Screws are usually included, but allowance should be made for any waste (loss say add minimum 1% to P C sum).

7.4 UNIT RATE CALCULATIONS

Examples are now given of typical unit rate calculations for woodwork.

Table 7.18 Unit rate calculation for carcassing

Item			Rate	Extension	Total
7.1		Sawn softwood 50 × 200 mm in floors.		($£/m^3$)	($£/m$)
	Materials				
	1 m³	Softwood carcassing		226.00	
		Unload: labourer 0.50 hours	3.90	1.95	
				227.95	
		Waste	7½%	17.10	
	5 kg	Nails (including waste)	0.60	3.00	
				248.05	
	Labour				
	21 MH	Carpenter	5.43	114.03	
		0.050 × 0.200 @		362.08	3.62
7.2		50 × 100 mm in pitched roofs.			
	Materials				
	1 m³	Softwood carcassing		220.00	
		Unload: labourer 0.50 hours	3.90	1.95	
				221.95	
		Waste	7½%	16.65	
		Nails as before		3.00	
				241.60	
	Labour				
	30 MH	Carpenter	5.43	162.90	
		0.050 × 0.100 @		404.50	2.02

Where timber is quoted at a price per lineal metre, for carcassing items it will be found best to convert to a price per cubric metre for calculation purposes. Thus, 50 × 100 carcassing timber @ £1.10 per lineal metre equals £220.00 per cubic metre.

Table 7.19 Unit rate calculation for first fixings

Item			Rate	Extension	Total
				$£/m^2$	
7.3	Boardings and Flooring—Softwood. Tongued and grooved wrought board flooring 25 mm thick; 150 mm widths.				
	Materials	($£/100$ m)			
		25×150 PTG	96.00		
		100 m $= 0.375$ m^3			
		Unload 0.5 hrs $\times 0.375$ m^3 @ 3.90	0.73		
			96.73		
				($£/100$ m)	($£/m^2$)
	1 m^2	Length required per m^2 $= \dfrac{1\,\text{m} \times 1\,\text{m}}{140\,\text{mm (nett width)}} = 7.14$ m	96.73	6.906	
	65 mm	nails $\dfrac{7.14 \times 2\,\text{nails/joist}}{400\,\text{mm (centres of joists)}} = 36$			
		36 nails @ $240/\text{kg} = 0.15$ kg	0.56	0.084	
				6.990	
		Cutting waste on boards and loss on nails	5%	0.349	
				7.339	
	Labour				
	0.60 MH	Carpenter	5.43	3.258	
				10.597	10.60
7.4	First Fixings—				
		Wrought Softwood 25×150 fascia.			
	Materials		($£/100$ m)	($£/m$)	($£/m$)
	1 m	25×150 planed all round	121.00	1.21	
		Waste	$7\frac{1}{2}$%	0.09	
				1.30	
		Nails nominal		0.05	
				1.35	
	Labour				
	0.25	Carpenter hours	5.43	1.36	
				2.71	2.71

Table 7.19 (*Contd.*)

Item		Rate	Extension	Total
7.5 *First Fixings —*				
	Sawn Softwood		(£/100m)	(£/m)
	25 × 50 grounds plugged to brickwork			
Materials				
100 m	25 × 50 sawn softwood			29.600
	Waste	7½%		2.220
				31.820
	Nails and plugs			
	100 m ÷ 400 mm = 250 No.	0.02		5.000
	Waste	10%		0.500
				37.320
Labour				
(MH/m)				
0.07	Fix ground			
0.12	Plug			
0.19	× 100 m = 19 MH	5.43	103.17	1.40
				140.49

In this case the cost for 100 m of grounds has been calculated since the price quoted for supply is per 100 m and the number of plugs can be more easily calculated.

Table 7.20 Unit rate calculation for second fixings

Item		Rate	Extension	Total
7.6	*Unframed Second fixings—Wrought Softwood.*			
	19 × 50 Architraves			
Materials			(£/m)	(£/m)
1 m	19 × 50			0.34
	Waste	7½%		0.03
				0.37
	Nails nominal			0.03
				0.40
Labour				
0.10	Carpenter hours	5.43		0.54
				0.94	0.94

Table 7.21 Unit rate calculation for composite items

Item	Ouptut		Rate	Extension	Total
7.7		Doors–wrought softwood 44 mm External quality solid core flush door size 883 × 1981 mm covered both sides with ply wood and hardwood lipped on all edges			
	Material			(£/No.)	(£/No.)
	1 N^r	44 × 883 × 1981 solid core door		46.00	
		Waste–nominal	1%	0.46	46.46
	Labour				
	0.10 h	Labourer	3.90	0.39	
	2 hrs	Carpenter handle and fix (including butt hinges)	5.43	10.86	11.25
					57.91

SELF-ASSESSMENT QUESTIONS

Calculate nett unit rates for the following items using current costs for materials and labour.

1. 50 × 150 mm sawn softwood carcassing timber in floors. (£?/m)

2. 50 × 100 mm sawn softwood carcassing timber in partitions. (£?/m)

3. 25 mm tongued and grooved boards in 100 mm (nominal) widths, each board nailed with two 65 mm oval nails to each joist. (£?/m^2)

4. 64 × 100 mm door frame in wrought softwood, moulded, rebated and plugged to brick wall. (£?/m)

5. 25 × 75 mm *Oak* splayed skirting, plugged to brickwork and fixed with steel screws including sinking heads and pellating. (£?/m)

8

DRAINAGE

CHAPTER OBJECTIVES

After studying this chapter you should be able to:

- appreciate the main factors that affect the cost of items of drainage work;
- perform calculations based on representative examples.

8.1 CLASSIFICATION

The drainage section in the Standard Method of Measurement includes the following types of work: pipe trenches, including excavation, beds, benchings and coverings; pipework of clay, plastic and metal; manholes, soakaways, cesspits and septic tanks.

8.2 INTRODUCTION

It should be remembered that this work consists of a number of different trades and will be carried out by general labourers, concretors, pipelayers, bricklayers and plumbers, as necessary. Frequent reference will thus have to be made to previous chapters.

8.3 PIPE TRENCHES

8.3.1 Notes on calculating the cost of pipe trenches

1. Use outputs similar to those in 'excavations and earthwork'.
2. Allow for earthwork supports as dictated by site conditions
3. In these examples, earthwork support has been taken to apply to trenches over 1 metre deep.

4. It has also been assumed that any surplus spoil arising from the trenches can be spread and levelled adjacent to the trenches. This is practicable on, say, small housing schemes where the runs are shallow and short. On large contracts, and in other circumstances such as excavating through grassed or paved areas, the surplus soil remaining after backfill will have to be carted away. The quantity may amount to some 20–40% of the total volume excavated.
5. If it is necessary to cart away the surplus spoil, additional cost will be incurred which will vary as the distance to tip.
6. The width of trenches depends on the depth of trench, the diameter of pipe, whether hand or machine excavation is used and the type, if any, of earthwork support.

   For pipes up to and including 200 mm diameter take the widths to be as indicated in Table 8.1.

Table 8.1 Widths of trenches

	Width	
Depths	By hand	By machine
Not exceeding 1 m	500 mm	600 mm
Not exceeding 2 m	700 mm	800 mm
Not exceeding 4 m	900 mm	1000 mm

For pipes exceeding 200 mm diameter, increase the trench width in proportion to the increase in pipe diameter. Where a trench is machine excavated, take into account the width of excavator bucket available.
7. Note SMM clause W 3.1—depth range to be stated in increments of 2 m, and the average depth within the depth range to the nearest 0.25 m. The estimator may however be able to determine that trenches not exceeding an average depth of 750 mm will be within a depth range of 1 m. This is important, since it affects both the width of the trench and the time allowed to excavate it.
8. Wherever possible excavation and backfill will be by means of a machine. But in certain circumstances the work may have to be carried out by hand, for example where work is inside buildings; close to buildings; in wooded areas; electric or other services are in close proximity; steep ground slopes; short lengths; and where the cost of transporting machines to and from the site makes the work uneconomic.

8.3.2 Calculating unit rates for pipe trenches

It is suggested that the following procedure should be adopted when calculating unit rates for pipe trenches:

1. Calculate unit rates for each cost element.
2. Apply these unit rates to a 1 metre length of trench.
3. The technique of 'pro-rata' calculations may be adopted to save time when a number of trenches of increasing depth have to be calculated. However caution should be observed in order take due account of any relevant variable costs.

8.3.3 Pipe trenches—hand work

The following rates for each element are obtained with reference to the rates previously calculated for excavation and earthwork. Space is provided for you to add current rates if you wish.

	(MH/m³)	@£3.90/hr (£/m³)	Current rate (£/m³)
Excavate trenches:			
not exceeding 1.00 m deep	3.50	13.65	
not exceeding 2.00 m deep	4.50	17.55	
not exceeding 4.00 m deep	6.50	25.35	
Backfill and compact in layers	1.50	5.85	
Disposal of surplus spoil:			
If spread and levelled adjacent	1.25	4.87	
If removed from site calculate relevant cost			
	(MH/m)	(£/m)	(£/m)
Level and compact bottom of excavation	0.10	0.39	
Earthwork supports:			
As rates previously calculated —assumed in the examples given that open supports at 600 mm centres are required to trenches *over* 1 metre deep.		(£/m²)	
Maximum depth not exceeding 2 m (as item 4.8)		3.96	
Maximum depth not exceeding 4 m		?	

Examples are now given of the application of these elemental rates to the calculation of unit rates for pipe trenches.

Table 8.2 Unit rate calculation for excavating trenches by hand

Item				Rate	Extension	Total
		To receive pipes not exceeding 200 mm diameter, grading bottoms; earthwork support; filling with excavated material and compacting; disposal of surplus spoil by spreading on site adjacent to excavation. Starting from ground level and not exceeding 2 m deep; average depth:			(£/m)	
8.1	0.75 m	Volume 1 m × 500 × 750	0.375 m³			
		Excavate		13.65★	5.119	
		Level and compact	1 m	0.39	0.390	
		Earthwork support (not required)		—	—	
		Backfill 75%	0.281 m³	5.85	1.644	
		Disposal 25%	0.094 m³	4.87	0.458	
					7.611	7.61
8.2	1.00 m	Volume 1 m × 500 × 1000	0.50 m³			
		Excavate (assumed not exceeding 1 m deep)		13.65★	6.825	
		Level and compact		0.39	0.390	
		Earthwork support		—	—	
		Backfill 75%	0.375 m³	5.85	2.194	
		Disposal 25%	0.125 m³	4.87	0.609	
					10.018	10.02
8.3	1.25 m	Volume 1 m × 700 × 1.250	0.875 m³			
		Excavate (note change in rate)		17.55	15.356	
		Level and compact		0.39	0.390	

Table 8.2 (*Contd.*)

Item				Rate	Extension	Total
					(£/m)	
		Earthwork support				
		2 × 1 × 1.25	2.50 m²	3.96	9.900	
		Backfill 75%	0.656 m³	5.85	3.838	
		Disposal 25%	0.219 m³	4.87	1.066	
					30.550	30.55
8.4	2.00 m	Volume				
		1 m × 700 × 2 000	1.40 m³			
		Excavate		17.55	24.570	
		Level and compact	1 m	0.39	0.390	
		Earthwork support				
		2 × 1 × 2	4 m²	3.96	15.840	
		Backfill 75%	1.05 m³	5.85	6.142	
		Disposal 25%	0.35 m³	4.87	1.704	
					48.646	48.65

Intermediate depths may be
derived by the pro-rata method
as in the following examples:

	Depth (m)	Rate (£)		
	2.00	48.65		
	1.25	30.55		
Difference	0.75	18.10	∴ £6.03 per 250 mm	stage
	1.25	30.55		
	1.50	36.58		
	1.75	42.61		
	2.00	48.65		

★ assumed trench does not in fact exceed 1 m in depth.

8.3.4 Pipe trenches—machine work

	(£/hr)	Current rate (£/hr)
JCB3c, or similar:		
Hire rate including fuel and operator	11.00	
Banksman (Labourers rate 3.90 + 0.10)	4.00	
	15.00	

		(m³/hr)	@£15.00 (£/m³)	Current rate (£/m³)
Excavate trenches:				
Not exceeding 2 m deep	(3–10%)	2.70	5.55	
Not exceeding 4 m deep		3.00	5.00	
Backfill		4.00	3.75	
Disposal of surplus spoil:				
Spread and level adjacent		5.00	3.00	
Disposal—calculate relevant cost				

Table 8.3 presents two typical examples of the calculation of unit rates for pipe trenches where machines are used. You should see that the procedure is similar to that of hand excavation, but that usually the trenches are wider, as noted in a previous table.

Table 8.3 Unit rate calculation for excavating trenches by machine

Item				Rate	Extension	Total
		To receive pipes not exceeding 200 mm diameter, grading bottoms, earthwork support, filling with excavated material and compacting, disposal of surplus soil by spreading on site adjacent to excavation. Starting from ground level and not exceeding 2 m deep; average depth:			(£/m)	
8.5	0.75 m	Volume				
		1 m × 600 × 750	0.45 m³			
		Excavate		5.55	2.497	
		Level and compact	1 m	0.39	0.390	
		Earthwork support (not required)	—	—	—	
		Backfill 75%	0.34 m³	3.75	1.275	
		Disposal 25%	0.11 m³	3.00	0.330	
					4.492	4.49
8.6	1.00 m	Volume				
		1 m × 600 × 1	0.60 m³			
		Excavate (assumed not exceeding 1 m deep)		5.55	3.330	
		Level and compact	1 m	0.36	0.390	
		Earthwork support (not required)	—	—	—	
		Backfill 75%	0.45 m³	3.75	1.687	
		Disposal 25%	0.15 m³	2.94	0.450	
					5.857	5.86

Table 8.4 Unit rate calculation for granular beds and surrounds

Item			Rate	Extension	Total
	Priced in a similar manner to hardcore fill, i.e. by the metre cube initially, however the labour content and wastage is usually greater due to the dispersed nature of the work.				
8.7	Granular material in regulating bed average 100 mm thick laid in bottom of trench under UPVC drain pipe.				
	Materials		(£/t)	(£/m³)	
	1 m³ Granular material 1700 kg		4.60	7.82	
	Waste (often badly misused on site) 33⅓%			2.61	
				10.43	
	Labour	(MH/m³)			
	Load barrow	1.00			
	Wheel	2.00 (say 50 m average)			
	Place	1.00			
		4.00 Labourer	3.90	15.60	
				26.03	
	Volume per lineal metre				
	100 mm thick		(£/m³)		(£/m)
	× 600 mm★ wide = 0.60 m³		26.03		1.56
8.8	Granular material in surround to 100 mm diameter UPVC drain pipe laid in trench to a depth of 100 mm above crown of pipe.				
	Volume per lineal metre		(£/m³)		(£/m)
	1 m × 600 mm★ × 200 mm = 0.12 m³		26.03		3.12

★Note that in the last two items the width of the trench has been taken as 600 mm, if the trench is a different width this will affect the volume of gravel required correspondingly. Further in the last item due to the small diameter of the pipe it has not been thought necessary to make any deduction for the volume of the pipe.

8.4 CONCRETE: BEDS, BEDS AND BENCHINGS, BEDS AND COVERINGS

These are all priced in a similar manner to in-situ concrete foundations. However, usually a much higher labour content is involved, since the concrete is generally in smaller quantities and long lengths of drains increase distribution costs. The waste allowance should be increased to at least 10%.

Table 8.5 Concrete volume per lineal metre

Diameter of pipe	Bed only		Bed and benching		Square section surround	
	(100mm)	(150mm)	(100mm)	(150mm)	(100mm)	(150mm)
100	0.050	0.075	0.070	0.095	0.150	0.200
150	0.055	0.083	0.080	0.108	0.190	0.240
225	0.063	0.094	0.095	0.126	0.260	0.320

Table 8.5 gives an indication of the volume of concrete required per lineal metre. All concrete beds are taken to be 400mm *wider* than the pipe diameter—adjust the above figures for other widths. The price per cubic metre of concrete may be calculated as follows, and then applied to the above volumes to obtain the required unit rates.

Concrete (1:3:6)

			($\pounds$/m^3)
Materials:			
Mix 1:3:6 as previous calculation in concretor			25.68
Waste: 5% included nett $= \dfrac{100}{105} \times 25.68$			24.46
allow		10%	2.45
			26.91

Labour:	(MH/m^3)			
Mix	2.00	(100 litre mixer)		
Wheel	2.00	(say 50m average)		
Place	2.00			
	6.00		3.90	23.40
				50.31

These man hours may be compared with the output standards, in concretor (Chapter 5), for plain concrete in foundations, and may be reduced if a dumper is used to convey the concrete. In certain circumstances formwork may be required, and this cost will then have to be added to the item.

8.5 PIPEWORK

Three types of pipe are considered:

1. vitrified spigot and socketed clay pipes with rigid cement and sand joints;

2. vitrified clay pipes with plain ends and flexible couplings;
3. plastic (UPVC) pipes with ring seal sockets.

8.5.1 Cost comparisons

When working out cost comparisons the following points should be considered:

Clay pipes with rigid cement joints may be very difficult, if not impossible, to lay in waterlogged trenches.

Clay pipes with flexible couplings obviate the above problem and have the advantage of not being affected by small ground movements.

Plastic pipes are very easy to handle, cut and lay in very long lengths, but they require the addition of a granular bed and surround, and are thus more expensive in total.

Relative changes in material prices may change the price conclusions given below.

8.5.2 Vitrified socketed clay pipes and fittings to BS 65 for cement mortar joints

Prices for British Standard Surface Water Quality are given in Table 8.6.

Table 8.6 Pipe prices

Diameter	100 mm	150 mm	225 mm	300 mm
Price per metre (£)	1.58	2.90	5.66	10.31

British Standard 'Normal' quality pipes are plus 10%.

The above prices include for delivery within a certain distance from the works (Area 1). Other areas at a greater distance are necessarily at higher prices.

Small loads

A typical suppliers charging basis is as follows:

Loads over £1500		List
Loads under £1500 and over £1000	+	2½%
Loads under £1000 and over £750	+	7½%
Loads under £750 and over £500	+	17½%
Loads under £500 and over £250	+	25%
Loads under £250 and over £100	+	30%

Lengths

The standard length is 610 mm, but pipes are often available 1 m long. 150 mm pipes are available 1.40 m long and 225 mm pipes 1.60 m long.

Labour

Pipelayers and jointers receive extra payments for extra skill say 30 p per hour (above a labourer's rate). i.e. £3.90 + 30 p = £4.10 per hour. Bricklayers often carry out this work on small sites.

Typical outputs (hours per metre for 610 mm long pipes)

Table 8.7 Typical outputs

Diameter	100 mm	150 mm	225 mm
Unload	0.02	0.025	0.03
Lay (over 3 m long)	0.10	0.14	0.20
(under 3 m long)	0.15	0.20	0.30

Outputs are given in Table 8.7. These outputs are affected by the individual lengths of pipe, i.e.

- for 1.00 m long pipes reduce time allowance by 15%;
- for 1.40 m long pipes reduce time allowance by 20%;
- for 1.60 m long pipes reduce time allowance by 25%.

Short lengths

The SMM states that pipes in runs not exceeding 3 m long shall be so described stating the number. This is because such short lengths require up to 50% more time to lay than lengths over 3 m.

Jointing—materials and labour

See Table 8.8.

Table 8.8 Jointing outputs

Diameter	100 mm	150 mm	225 mm
Yarn	0.02 kg	0.02 kg	0.07 kg
Cement mortar	0.0006 m^3	0.001 m^3	0.002 m^3
Labour hours	0.10	0.12	0.15

Waste

Allow for 5% waste due to breakages in handling and for cutting to length.

8.5.3 Vitrified clay drain pipes to BS 65 with plain ends and flexible polypropylene sleeve couplings

Typical outputs (hours per metre)

See Table 8.9.

Table 8.9 Typical outputs

Diameter	100 mm		150 mm	
Lenght (m)	1.00	1.60	1.00	1.75
Unload (hr)	0.02	0.02	0.025	0.025
Lay and joint (hr)	0.15	0.14	0.20	0.18

These pipes are available in diameters of 100, 150, 200 and 225 mm. Lengths vary.
Waste: allow 5%

8.5.4 Vitrified clay drain pipes to BS 65 with spigot and socket and flexible polyester ring joints

These pipes are available in diameters of 100 mm to 800 mm inclusive. Typical outputs are similar to the pipes with plain ends and flexible sleeves—probably less 10%.

8.5.5 UPVC drain pipes to BS 4660 with ring seal sockets

Typical outputs—(hours per metre)

Table 8.10 Typical outputs

Diameter	100 mm		150 mm	
Length	3 m	6 m	3 m	6 m
Unload (hr)	0.01	0.01	0.01	0.01
Lay and joint (hr)	0.07	0.06	0.09	0.07

8.5.6 Unit rate calculations

Examples are now given of the calculation of unit rates for three typical items.

Table 8.11 Unit rate calculations for pipework

Item		Rate	Extension	Total
	Vitrified socketed clay pipes and fittings to BS 65 with tarred gaskin and cement mortar joints.			
8.9	100 mm 'normal quality' pipes in runs over 3 m long			
	Materials		(£/m)	(£/m)
	1 100 mm pipe; standard list in 1 m lengths		1.580	
	Normal quality	+ 10%	0.158	
			1.738	
	Extra for small load (say under £250 over £100)	+ 30%	0.521	
			2.259	
	Waste	5%	0.113	
			2.372	
	Jointing materials:			
	gaskin 0.02 kg★	1.00	0.020	
	cement mortar 0.0006 m³★	36.00	0.034	2.426
	Labour			
	MH			
0.02	Unload	3.90	0.078	
0.085	Lay: since in 1 m lengths 0.10 − 15% = 0.085	4.10	0.348	
0.10	Joint	4.10	0.410	0.836
				3.262
	say			£3.26
8.10	Vitrified pipes to BS 65 with plain ends and flexible couplings. 100 mm in runs over 3 m long.			
	Materials		(£/m)	(£)
	1 m 100 mm pipe includes one coupling per length of pipe		1.630	

Table 8.11 (*Contd.*)

Item			Rate	Extension	Total
		Extra for loads under £500 and over £250	+25%	0.407	
				2.037	
		Waste	5%	0.102	2.139
	Labour (MH/m)				
	0.02	Unload	3.90	0.078	
	0.14	Lay and joint (1.60 m lengths)	4.10	0.574	0.652
					2.791
		say			2.79
8.11		Extra over 100 mm pipe for bend			
	Materials			(£/each)	(£/each)
		Bend includes one coupling		2.100	
		Extra for loads under £500 and over £250	+25%	0.525	
				2.625	
		Waste	5%	0.131	2.756
	Labour (MH)				
	0.02	Unload ⎱ Taken as equal to ⎰ 1 metre of pipe	3.90	0.078	
	0.15	Lay and joint ⎰	4.10	0.615	0.693
					3.449
		Less 0.33 m of pipe	2.79		0.921
					2.528
		say			2.53

*Including allowance for waste.

8.5.7 Testing

The cost of testing is related to the method of testing and the total length of drain pipes and number of manholes. The tests may be:

- air;
- smoke;
- hydraulic;

or a combination of these tests.

The tests may be required after the trenches are backfilled, but it may be considered prudent also to test prior to this, since it will be cheaper to rectify any defective drainage at this stage. It may be necessary to allow for the risk of failure and the cost of rectification.

SELF-ASSESSMENT QUESTIONS

Calculate nett unit rates for the following items using current costs for materials, plant and labour.

1. Excavate trenches to receive pipes not exceeding 200 mm diameter, grading bottoms, earthwork support, filling with excavated material and compacting, disposal of surplus spoil by spreading on site adjacent to excavation.

   (a) average 1.5 m deep (by hand); (£?/m)
   (b) average 2 m deep (by machine). (£?/m)

2. Granular material in regulating bed average 150 mm thick laid in bottom of trench under uPVC drain pipe. (£?/m)

3. Vitrified clay drain pipes to BS 65 with plain ends and flexible couplings. 150 mm in runs over 3 m long. (£?/m)

4. Vitrified clay drain pipes to BS 65 with plain ends and flexible couplings. 150 mm in runs not exceeding 3 m long. (£?/m)

   Information: an order of between £500 and £750 is expected to be placed for drainage goods.

9

PRICING SUB-CONTRACT WORK

CHAPTER OBJECTIVES

After studying this chapter you should be able to:

- appreciate the importance of the role of sub-contractors in the construction industry;

- differentiate between the different types of sub-contractors;

- appreciate the supervision and attendance on sub-contractors that may be required, and understand how its cost may be compiled.

9.1 SUB-CONTRACTING

It is common practice for general or main contractors to sub-let significant portions of the work to sub-contractors (referred to in contract terms as either domestic sub-contractors or nominated sub-contractors). Essentially this is done because the work can be carried out at a lower cost, or because it is of a specialized nature, which the main contractor cannot attempt to carry out using his own labour force. The advantages of sub-contracting include: minimization of risk borne by the main contractor, as the sub-contractor will give a fixed price for the sub-let work; and a saving in estimators' time, since there is no necessity to estimate the cost of the sub-contract work in detail. There is still the risk of the sub-contractor going into liquidation, or the architect refusing (with valid reason) to accept the sub-contractor, thus probably causing the contractor additional expense. Further the work is financed by sub-contractors and this can allow the main contractor to use his available finance for larger or other projects.

9.1.1 Types of sub-contractors

There are essentially two types of sub-contractors:

1. *Nominated sub-contractors*, i.e. specialist sub-contractors selected by the architect;
2. *Domestic sub-contractors* selected by the main contractor, and who may supply labour and materials, or labour only, for sections of the work.

An alternative, sometimes adopted, is for the architect to limit the selection to a few named sub-contractors. The successful firm, however, is still a domestic sub-contractor. In all cases the sub-contract terms of contract are signed between the sub-contractor and the main contractor, with the main contractor being responsible for supervision and payment in accordance with the main contract conditions.

9.1.2 Work by others directly engaged by the employer

It is important to note that the employer (client) may engage others directly to carry out part of the work, such as the installation of machines in a factory during the contract period.

In this case, the contractor's only obligation is by way of providing specified attendance which should be measured, or itemized and described in the bills of quantities in accordance with clause B.9 of the Standard Method of Measurement.

9.1.3 Trend towards more work being sub-contracted

Sub-contractors carry out a very high percentage of all construction work. For example, if we consider the cost analysis for the hypothetical three-storey office building referred to previously, the value of the work probably sub-contracted amounts to approximately 60% of the total contract sum. There is also a current trend towards more work being sub-contracted as construction becomes more complex, and more specialists are needed. Further, with labour costs rising, and the current difficulties of maintaining a constant flow of work, contractors are increasingly employing sub-contractors who provide labour only.

It should not be thought, however, that sub-contracting absolves the main contractor of responsibility for the contract performance. Reasons for not sub-contracting may include:

- Difficulty in keeping sub-contractors to the desired programme;

- The possible financial failure of the sub-contractor, leading to increased cost and probably extensions of contract duration;
- The quality of workmanship being difficult to maintain;
- The high level of supervision required by the main contractor to keep control of quality and programme.

The various types of sub-contractors are now described, and details are given of the factors that should be considered at the tender stage by the estimator.

9.2 NOMINATED SUB-CONTRACTORS

Clause 35 of the JCT Form of Contract 1980 deals with nominated sub-contractors.

The architect has the right, under this clause, to select a sub-contractor either by the use of a prime cost sum, or by the naming of a sole sub-contractor in the bills of quantities. The contractor may be permitted to tender for such work by the architect where, as is usual, a prime cost sum is stated.

Where Clause 35.3 is operated, involving the following documents issued by the Joint Contracts' Tribunal:

- Tender NSC/1
- Agreement NSC/2
- Nomination NSC/3
- Sub-contract NSC/4

then the nominated sub-contractor has the opportunity of agreeing with the main contractor a schedule of programme details and attendance proposals prior to the issue of a nomination instruction by the architect.

Thus the contractor should ensure that his pre-tender construction programme is realistic in making a suitable time allowance for not only his own work but that of both domestic and nominated sub-contractors. The nominated sub-contractor should set out his programme requirements on NSC/1, Schedule 1 at tender stage. Where clause 35.11 is operated Tender NSC/1 and Agreement NSC/2 are not used:

- Agreement NSC/2a
- Sub-contract NSC/4a

may apply, NSC/2a being used where design work by, or early final or direct payment to, the sub-contractor are required. The alternative method of nomination, however, must use form NSC/4a. It is the architect's responsibility to provide, and the estimator's responsibility to recognize, whether adequate information is available relating to the prospective nomination.

The following extract from a bill of quantities shows the usual

Table 9.1 Typical extract from a bill of quantities:

Nominated sub-contractors		£
Allow the prime cost sum of £92500.00		
for structural steel work		92 500.00
Profit	%	
General attendance	Item	
Other attendance:		
Providing power 110 volt AC		
Providing temporary hard surface to the whole of the working area and access thereto, suitable for the passage of 32 tonne gross weight loaded vehicles and pneumatic tyred mobile cranes	Item	

information given at the tender stage to the estimator. If the name of the proposed nominated sub-contractor is known at this stage, then it should also be stated.

It will be noted that in the example shown in Table 9.1 the extent of general attendance is not defined, since an all embracing definition is given in the Standard Method of Measurement. Other attendance has, however, been specifically stated, since this will vary according to the type of work and the requirements of the nominated sub-contractor.

9.2.1 General attendance

As defined in clause B 9.2 of the Standard Method of Measurement, 'general attendance' covers: the use of the contractors' temporary roads, standing scaffolding, standing power operated hoisting plant; the provision of temporary lighting and water supplies; clearing away rubbish; provision of space for the sub-contractor's own offices and stores; and the use of canteen, sanitary accommodation and other welfare facilities.

9.2.2 Other attendance

Any 'other attendance', previously called 'special attendance', to be provided specifically for a sub-contractor has to be either specified in the bills of quantities under item B 9.3 of the Standard Method of Measurement, or in the case of domestic sub-contractors may be a condition of the quotation.

Examples of 'other attendance' are: special scaffolding requirements, either being scaffolding that is not required by the main contractor or scaffolding required to be left up (and maintained) for an extended period of time; and the provision of access roads or hardstanding specifically for the use of the sub-contractor.

9.3 DOMESTIC SUB-CONTRACTORS

Domestic Sub-contractors are selected by the main contractors, but have to be approved in writing by the architect (which approval shall not be unreasonably withheld) under Clause 19 (Assignment and Sub-contracts) of the JCT form.

Sometimes as mentioned previously, the contract bills may provide that certain work must be carried out by persons selected by the contractor from a list of at least three persons. This list may, however, be added to by the contractor with the approval of the architect.

There may be a hundred or more domestic sub-contractors on a large or complex contract. However, as can be seen from the typical contractor's cost breakdown of an office block in Chapter 2, the most usual would include the work of roofing, plastering, wall tiling, floor finishes, painting and decorating.

Several sub-contractors should be requested to submit competitive tenders, and should be chosen on the basis of past performance for quality, keeping to programme, and finally by price.

9.4 LABOUR-ONLY SUB-CONTRACTING

Labour only sub-contractors as their name suggests, provide a labour force for particular sections of the work, such as concreting or bricklaying. The main contractor provides all the necessary materials including, usually, any necessary unloading and distribution. Waste may be even greater than usual since, as the basis for payment to the sub-contractor is usually on a schedule of labour-only rates or a fixed price, economy in the use of materials will not be uppermost in the sub-contractor's mind.

The section later in this chapter which deals with the construction industry tax deduction scheme is particularly relevant to labour-only sub-contracting.

9.5 CONSTRUCTION MANAGEMENT

In many cases of large construction projects, the main contractor supplies little or no labour of his own and acts solely in a construction management capacity, so that his main direct costs are contained in the project overheads element. All the construction work in this event is sub-contracted.

9.5.1 Factors affecting cost

The factors affecting cost when employing sub-contractors, such as duration (programme), supervision and attendance, will now be considered.

Programme

Since the main contractor has either to agree to the contract period given in the tender documents, or determine the contract period himself, it follows that the duration of the individual sub-contract works is important, and may be critical to the overall contract period. Where the durations are critical, agreement of the sub-contract period or periods should be reached with the domestic sub-contractors. In the case of nominated sub-contractors, if the name of the sub-contractor is known and given in the bills of quantities (Clause B9.1), then an assessment of a suitable time may be requested prior to submission of the tender, otherwise, as mentioned previously, a reasonable period has to be assessed by the main contractor.

Supervision

The main contractor has to supervise all work, including that of sub-contractors, to see that: the programme, specification and drawings are adhered to. Thus a great deal of technical and management expertise may be involved, especially on complex and large contracts. A great amount of co-ordination will certainly be required so that the necessary staff and their time must be allowed for. Setting out to line and level of sub-contractor's work may be necessary, requiring the services of a site engineer.

Builder's work

Such work as cutting chases in brickwork, cutting or forming holes through walls and floors for pipes, forming ducts and chambers, is measured in detail in the bill of quantities and priced in the normal way.

Materials

Domestic sub-contractors such as plasterers and painters will normally provide *all* the materials necessary to complete their work. Roofers, on the other hand, although supplying roofing felt, battens, tiles, nails and clips, will usually expect the main contractor to provide any necessary sand and cement for bedding ridge tiles, etc.

Unloading

Materials for the sub-contractors may be delivered to the site prior to any of the sub-contractor's men arriving on site, and, therefore, the main contractor may undertake to unload, stack, and protect the materials as necessary. If the items are very heavy a fork lift or crane may have to be used. The sub-contract quotation should state if any such attendance is required, and, in that event, the cost should be calculated and allowed in the tender by the estimator.

Scaffolding

It should be noted that the Domestic Sub-Contract DOM/1 specifically requires the main contractor to provide scaffolding, if necessary, at no charge, over 3.30 m high.

9.5.2 Estimate of cost of supervision, materials and unloading

Supervision

Price in the project overheads and allocate in preliminaries section of bill of quantities

Materials

Applicable to domestic sub-contractors—add the cost to the relevant measured work items as quoted by the sub-contractor.

Unloading

Calculate the cost applicable to each sub-contractor and if necessary co-relate to the total for all sub-contract material and materials required for own forces. It may be necessary for example to have say one forklift and two labourers for a period of 40 weeks. The cost can then be allocated in the preliminaries and in the case of nominated sub-contractors in the relevant attendance items.

9.5.3 Summing up

The cost of supervision and general attendance is a normal cost to the main contractor and has always to be calculated and allowed for. Nominated sub-contractors may require 'other attendance', and this has to be priced in accordance with the relevant item description in the bill of quantities (SMM B9.3). Domestic and labour-only sub-contractor's quotations have to be carefully scrutinized for specific requirements, and any relevant additional costs to the main contractor ascertained.

9.6 CONSTRUCTION INDUSTRY TAX DEDUCTION SCHEME

The scheme applies to payments made by 'contractors' to 'sub-contractors', and is intended to eliminate tax avoidance by sub-contractors. If the 'sub-contractor' holds a tax certificate (Form 714) issued by the Inland Revenue, the 'contractor' pays the 'sub-contractor' in full. If the 'sub-contractor' does not hold a certificate, the 'contractor' should make a tax deduction* from the payment and pass it over to the Inland Revenue. A deduction note (Form SC60) is given by the 'contractor' to the 'sub-contractor' showing how much tax has been deducted, so that at the end of the year a reconciliation may be made with the Inspector of Taxes. If too much tax has been paid a rebate is made.

Advice on how to operate the scheme is contained in a booklet IR 14/15 (1982) issued by the Board of Inland Revenue. Whoever certifies and makes payments to sub-contractors must therefore be aware of this tax deduction scheme, since otherwise the contractor may be faced with an additional tax bill, and indeed prosecution, for not complying with the law.

9.7 PRICES FOR DOMESTIC SUB-CONTRACT WORK

It is recommended practice that quotations be obtained for all work which is to be sub-contracted. However, where this is not possible the builders' estimator has to prepare his own prices. When preparing these prices the following points should be borne in mind:

1. Is the work in small quantities?
2. Is the work of an intermittent nature due to the design or the construction programme of the main contractor's work?
3. What project overheads will be required; including supervision, plant and travelling time and expenses?
4. Due allowance must be made for general overheads and profit.

These factors may mean an addition of 15 to 50% or more on nett calculated rates. It will be appreciated that although material costs may be calculated fairly accurately, by a systematic breakdown of the work description, labour costs are an entirely different matter, since only the sub-contractor is in a position to collect accurate data on labour outputs and his project and general overheads.

Tables 9.2–9.10 present material and output data for the more usual domestic sub-contractors. These data will provide a basis for an appreciation of the costs involved in calculating selected unit rates.

*currently 30% of the labour value.

9.7.1 Roofing

See Tables 9.2–9.4.

Table 9.2

Item	Unit	Waste (%)	Unload and fix roofer and labourer (hours)
Roofing felt	100 m²	7.5	5
Battens 25 × 50	100 m	5	2
Ridge tiles	100 m	5	33

Table 9.3

Item	Unit	Unloading labourer (hours)	Fix roofer and labourer (hours)
Slates:			
660 × 406	1000	3.00	15.0
510 × 255	1000	2.00	12.5
355 × 200	1000	1.25	10.0
Plain tiles:			
266 × 165	1000	1.00	5.0
Interlocking tiles:			
380 × 230	1000	1.50	15.0
413 × 330	1000	2.25	19.0
430 × 380	1000	2.50	21.0
Corrugated sheet Roofing:			
Asbestos cement			
Standard 75 mm	100 m²	2.00	20.0

Waste allowance: slates and tiles 2½–5%

Table 9.4 Approximate number of nails per kilogramme

	Size (mm)	Copper	Aluminium alloy
Slating nails	38	370	350
	44	280	270
	50	220	210
		Galvanized	
Batten nails	50 × 10 g	260	
	63 × 10 g	220	

9.7.2 Floor, wall and ceiling finishings

Table 9.5 Output standards per m^2 for plain sheet finishings fixed to vertical wood framing by carpenters

Material			Nails/pins (kg)	Plain (man hours/m^2)
Hardboard	{	3 mm	0.03	0.30
	{	6 mm	0.03	0.35
Fibre	{	12 mm	0.07	0.30
Insulation board	{	18 mm	0.08	0.35
	{	6 mm	0.05	0.35
Plywood	{	9 mm	0.06	0.40
	{	12 mm	0.07	0.45
Blockboard	{	12 mm	0.07	0.45
or chipboard	{	18 mm	0.08	0.50
Asbestos cement		6 mm	0.06	0.60

The man hours indicated in Table 9.5 include for all normal handling on site.

Variations on above man hours

Prefinished/veneered	+ 50%
Fixed to soffits	+ 15%
Fixed to floors	− 25%
Glued and pinned	+ 25%
Screwed	+ 50%

For very large areas with negligible cutting the man hours can be reduced by up to 50%.

Waste

Allow at least 5% for waste, except on small jobs when due to extra cutting 15% or more may be necessary. This factor is highly variable, it is most important to find out the floor to ceiling height when used as wall lining and relate to standard size sheets available. Also depends if finished surface or covered by other materials.

In-situ finishings

See Table 9.6.

Table 9.6 Output standards per m² for in-situ finishings

The following work to walls: to brickwork or blockwork base	(Man hours)
Mortar; first and finishing coat of cement and sand; steel trowelled; 19 mm	
over 300 mm wide	0.75
not exceeding 300 mm wide	1.25
Tyrolean decorative rendering: 13 mm first coat of cement, lime and sand (1:1:6); finishing, three coats of Cullamix applied with hand-operated machine.	
over 300 mm wide	0.90
not exceeding 300 mm wide	1.50
Plaster; first and finishing coat of 'Carlite' premixed lightweight plaster; steel trowelled; 13 mm;	
over 300 mm wide	0.50
not exceeding 300 mm wide	0.85
Plaster; one coat 'Snowplast' plaster; steel trowelled; 13 mm;	
over 300 mm wide	0.45
not exceeding 300 mm wide	0.75
The following work to ceilings; to plaster board base 'Thistle' board finish plaster; steel trowelled; 5 mm one coat; including scrimming joints;	
over 300 mm wide	0.40
not exceeding 300 mm wide	0.65

Material standards

Prices for the required mortars may be calculated in accordance with the methods indicated in the brickwork and blockwork section. An addition of 33⅓% should be made for: compression, keying into the joints of the brick or blockwork and waste.

The quantities shown in Table 9.7 will vary depending on the nature and accuracy of the backing.

Table 9.7 Material standards for in-situ finishings

Plasters		(kg/m²)
'Carlite' browning		6
'Carlite' finish	total 13 mm	2
'Thistle' board finish	5 mm	4
'Snowplast' gypsum plaster	13 mm	10

Table 9.8 Output standards for in-situ finishings 1

Plasterwork sundries	Unit	(Man hours)
Arris	m	0.10
Fair edge and arris	m	0.15
Make good to pipes, etc.		
not exceeding 0.30 m girth	No.	0.10
over 0.30 not exceeding 1 m girth	No.	0.20
Angle bead	m	0.10

Table 9.9 Output standards for in-situ finishings 2

Plasterboard	Unit	(Man hours)
Lath or baseboard fixed with nails;		
to receive plaster; to walls;		
over 300 mm wide	m²	0.15
not exceeding 300 mm wide	m²	0.25
Lath or baseboard fixed to ceilings;		
over 300 mm wide	m²	0.17
not exceeding 300 mm wide	m²	0.28
Tapered edge wallboard; filled and		
scrimmed joints; for direct decoration;		
to walls;		
over 300 mm wide	m²	0.30
not exceeding 300 mm wide	m²	0.50

Table 9.10 Output standards for in-situ finishings 3

Metal lath	Unit	(Man hours)
Metal lathing; fixing with staples to		
softwood; to walls;		
over 300 mm wide	m²	0.15
not exceeding 300 mm wide	m²	0.25
to ceilings;		
over 300 mm wide	m²	0.20
not exceeding 300 mm wide	m²	0.33
raking cutting	m	0.10

The allowance for laps may be calculated by considering the size of sheet available and the laps specified—usually 50 mm, to this should be added 2½–5% for cutting waste a total of 10–12½%.

> ## SELF-ASSESSMENT QUESTIONS

1. Differentiate between the two classifications of sub-contractors employed on building works.

2. Give an example of 'other attendance' and explain how this item should be priced.

3. What facilities will a sub-contractor for roofing work be likely to require?

4. If the builder's estimator has to prepare prices for work that is usually sub-contracted, what are typical factors that may have to be considered?

5. Using current prices, calculate a unit rate for the following item:

   Welsh blue slates 510×255 to sloping roof; 75mm lap fix with alloy nails, including 50×19 softwood battens (Quantity 60m^2) £?/m^2.

6. Work normally carried out by the main contractor includes: excavation work, formwork,concreting, reinforcement, brickwork and woodwork. This work may, however, be sub-contracted. Present the arguments for and against this.

10

DAYWORK

CHAPTER OBJECTIVES

After studying this chapter you should be able to:

- understand the composition of dayworks and distinguish between the definition of prime costs and the percentage additions;
- calculate the percentage additions for labour, materials and plant.

10.1 ALLOWANCE FOR UNFORESEEN WORKS

During the preparation of tender documents it is often required that allowance be made for work or for costs which cannot be entirely foreseen, defined or detailed. This eventuality is taken into account in a Bill of Quantities by allowing a provisional sum for dayworks. When unforeseen work occurs then the architect will issue a variation order and it will be valued by the quantity surveyor named in the contract.

10.2 PAYMENTS

The variations are valued in accordance with the contract (JCT 1980 Clause 13.5) and must, where possible, be measured and valued in relation to the Contract Bills of Quantities. If the work cannot be properly valued in this way, then the valuations will comprise the prime cost of such work, together with the appropriate percentage additions inserted in the Contract Bills by the contractor. Thus, the estimator has to read carefully the definitions of prime cost and then calculate the appropriate percentage additions.

10.3 CLASSIFICATION

Daywork may be classified as follows:

Daywork carried out under, and incidental to, a building contract. Daywork ordered to be carried out after the date of commencement of the defects liability period. This is subject to agreement as to terms since there is no obligation on the contractor to admit a variation order during the defects liability period.

Jobbing or any other work carried out as a main or separate contract. Depending upon the classification, the percentage required for recovery of overheads and profit will vary to take account of the different conditions under which the work will be carried out.

10.4 AGREEMENT WITH CLIENT

The contractor should reach agreement with the client on the definition of prime cost and the percentages to be used to cover overheads and profit *before* carrying out the work. Where the work is being carried out using the JCT Form of building contract, then the definition of day work will be given in the tender documents.

10.5 COMPOSITION OF TOTAL CHARGES

The example given is based upon the use of the JCT Form and upon the 'Definition of Prime Cost Daywork' prepared and published by the Royal Institution of Chartered Surveyors and the Building Employers Confederation.

The daywork account will include the following costs: labour; materials and goods; plant. To each of these costs is added a percentage addition for: incidental costs, overheads and profit. (This addition will vary for labour, materials and plant costs.)

Sub-contractors

It should be noted that the RICS has also agreed definitions of prime cost with the Electrical Contractors Association and the National Association of Plumbing, Heating and Mechanical Services Contractors. Other sub-contractors are not recognized for daywork purposes. The percentage addition must therefore include for any possible additional costs incurred when sub-contractors are employed on daywork.

10.6 PRIME COSTS AND PERCENTAGE ADDITION

The prime costs and percentage addition are now considered in greater detail.

10.6.1 Labour

The calculation for what is called the 'standard hourly base rate', in the definition of prime cost of daywork, does not include all the costs included in the usual calculation to arrive at the 'all-in hourly rate'. The exceptions are to be included in the percentage addition for incidental costs, overheads and profit.

Example of calculation of typical standard hourly base rate for building craftsman and labourer in Grade A areas at 4 August, 1986

	Rate £	Craftsman £	Rate £	Labourer £
Guaranteed minimum weekly earnings				
Standard basic rate 47.8 wks	98.28	4697.78	83.85	4008.03
Guaranteed minimum bonus 47.8 wks	15.21	727.04	12.87	615.19
		5424.82		4623.22
Employer's National Insurance contribution	9%	488.23	9%	416.09
Annual holidays with pay and retirement and death benefit scheme 47.0 wks	12.50	587.50		587.50
CITB annual levy		75.00		18.00
		6575.55		5644.81
Divide by standard working hours of 1801.8		£3.65		£3.13
Standard working hours calculated as follows:				
52 wks @ 39 hrs		2028.0		
Less: 4.8 wks holiday @ 39 hrs	163.8			
8 days public holiday @ 7.8 hrs	62.4	226.2		
		1801.8 hrs		

An addition should be made, where appropriate, for payments made under the Working Rule for:
   discomfort, inconvenience or risk;
   continuous extra skill or
   responsibility; intermittent
   responsibility.

Incidental costs, overheads and profit

The percentage adjustments provided in the building contract, which are applicable to each of the totals of labour, materials and plant, comprise the following:

- head office charges
- site staff, including site supervision
- the additional cost of overtime (other than authorized)
- time lost due to inclement weather★
- the additional cost of incentive payments above the guaranteed minimum★
- apprentices' study time
- subsistence and periodic allowances
- fares and travelling allowances
- sick pay or insurance in respect thereof★
- third party and employers' liability insurance★
- liability in respect of redundancy payments to employees★
- employers' National Insurance contributions★
- tool allowances★
- use, repair and sharpening of non-mechanical hand tools
- use of erected scaffolding or the like
- use of tarpaulins, protective clothing, artificial lighting, safety and welfare facilities available on site
- any variation to basic rates in relation to any specified schedule of basic plant charges
- all other liabilities and obligations whatsoever not specifically referred to in this section nor chargeable under any other section
- profit.

The cost of items marked with an asterisk★ is included in the calculation for the all-in labour rate (see Chapter 3).

Thus, if an allowance for the cost of the remaining items is added to the all-in hourly rate, the cost of employing labour on daywork should be obtained. In this case it is considered prudent to allow for the following additional costs:

	%
Head office charges	10
Site staff	15
Additional cost of overtime—only to be worked if authorized	—
Apprentices' study time (included in first item)	—
Subsistence (nil)	—
Fares	2
Use of non-mechanical hand tools	1
Use of erected scaffolding ⎫ nominal	
Use of tarpaulins ⎭	2

All other liabilities	10
Profit	10
	50

	Craftsman £	Labourer £
All-in hourly rate including incentive bonus of 33⅓%	4.55	3.91
Addition as above 50%	2.27	1.95
Daywork rate	6.82	5.86
Less standard base rate	3.65	3.13
Addition	3.17	2.73

Expressed as a percentage on standard base rate this addition becomes

for craftsmen $\dfrac{3.17}{3.65} \times 100 = 86.8\%$

for labourers $\dfrac{2.73}{3.13} \times 100 = 87.2\%$

Since one percentage only is required, a weighted average could be calculated on the assumption that there are two craftsmen to one labourer:

Daywork rate		£	
2 craftsmen	@ 6.82	13.64	
1 labourer	@ 5.86	5.86	
		19.50	
Less standard base rate			
2 craftsmen	@ 3.65	7.30	
1 labourer	@ 3.13	3.13	10.43
			9.07

Expressed as a percentage on the standard base rate

$\dfrac{9.07}{10.43} \times 100$ 87%

10.6.2 Materials and goods

Trade discounts are deducted but cash discounts not exceeding 5% may be retained.

An allowance should be made for:

		%
Head office overheads	nominal	3
Site staff (checker/storekeeper)	nominal	2
Profit		10
		15

10.6.3 Plant

The rates for the use of mechanical and non-mechanical plant shall be as provided in the contract—usually the RICS Schedule of Basic Plant Charges. The last and current publication (in 1986) was published 1 January, 1981.

To update the figures the following calculations may be made using the NEDO 'Plant' indices:

January 1981	191
April 1986	258
Change in indices	67

$$\frac{67}{191} \times 100 = 35\%$$

Since the application of the schedule is confined to plant already on the site, a simpler method may be for the estimator to compare the hire rates of plant to be used on site with the schedule rates. Say, in this case, the increase required amounts to 17%. Item (q) of incidental costs, overheads and profits makes provision for the eventuality of up-dating the stated rates in the percentage addition.

Thus:

		%
Head office overheads	nominal	3
Variation to basic rates (item (q))	allow	17
Profit		10
		30

Extract from bill of quantities

  Prime cost and provisional sums

Daywork		£
A Include the provisional sum of £1000.00 for labour		1000.00
B Add percentage addition	87%	870.00
C Include the provisional sum of £500.00 for materials and goods		500.00
D Add percentage addition	15%	75.00
E Include the provisional sum of £200.00 for plant		200.00
F Add percentage addition	30%	60.00
To collection		2705.00

It will be seen that the higher the percentage addition the higher the total included in the tender sum. Thus constraint is placed on the contractor to keep the percentage addition as low as possible in order to remain competitive.

10.7 DAYWORK ACCOUNTS

Daywork sheets will be prepared that detail the following: labour, with names and hours of workmen; materials and goods; plant. Each sheet will be signed by the contractor's representative and the clerk of works or other authorized person. These will be summarized by the quantity surveyor in a similar fashion to that shown.

  Specimen daywork account

	£	£
Labour	926.00	
Add 87%	805.62	1731.62
Materials and goods	396.00	
Add 15%	59.40	455.40
Plant	187.00	
Add 30%	56.10	243.10
Total for dayworks carried to summary		£2430.12

Spon's Architects' and Builders' Price Book gives detailed definitions of Daywork and Prime Cost including the Schedule of Basic Plant Charges published by the RICS. Details are also given of the daywork charges for the civil engineering industry prepared by the Federation of Civil Engineering Contractors. It is of interest to note that the suggested percentage additions, for civil engineering work, where no other rates have been agreed are: labour 133% and materials 12½%. However, the definitions are different and the conditions on civil engineering sites are very different.

SELF-ASSESSMENT QUESTIONS

1. Discuss the application of 'daywork' in the building industry.

2. Define the term 'standard hourly base rate' applied to dayworks.

3. Demonstrate how the percentage addition required on labour used for dayworks during the contract period should be calculated.

11

PROJECT OVERHEADS AND PRELIMINARIES

┌─────────────────────────┐
│ CHAPTER OBJECTIVES │
└─────────────────────────┘

After studying this chapter you should be able to:

- define the extent of project overheads on a typical contract;

- appreciate the importance of planning techniques in determining the extent of project overhead resources;

- price typical items—recognizing that the cost may be related to time or may be fixed.

11.1 PROJECT OVERHEADS

Project overheads are defined in the *Code of Estimating Practice* (CEP) as the cost of administering a project and providing general plant, site staff, facilities and site based services. A comprehensive schedule of project overheads is given in the Appendix to the CEP, and an example of priced project overheads for our hypothetical contract is given on the following pages.

The project overheads cannot be priced in detail until the construction programme, method statements and site layout diagram have been prepared; most of the items are time based and some, like temporary roads and hoardings, have to be measured.

11.2 PRELIMINARIES

The project overheads are often called 'preliminaries'. However, preliminaries are defined in the Standard Method of Measurement (SMM), and largely come under the heading of General Facilities and Obligations. Thus, there may be items in the preliminaries section of the bill of quantities that might influence the pricing generally, such as the names of the consultants, or the particular need to execute a section of the work by a specific time. In every case the preliminaries section of the bills of quantities should be closely scrutinized to ascertain which items need pricing and which items have a general effect.

Typical general facilities and obligations are:

- plant, tools and vehicles;
- scaffolding;
- site administration and security;
- transport for workpeople;
- protecting the works from inclement weather.

For the full list refer to SMM clause B.13. The list in the bill of quantities is very basic, and the general rule should be to price the project overheads in accordance with the Code of Estimating Practice and check to see what additional items require to be priced in the preliminaries section of the bill of quantities.

11.2.1 Proportion of contract costs

Project overheads seem to form an ever-increasing proportion of the total contract cost. This is due to such factors as: the increasing complexity of building which leads to the need for more highly trained supervision; greater use of machines requiring careful co-ordination (the cost of the machines, if used by more than one trade, is usually allocated in the preliminaries section of the bill of quantities); and increased standards of safety, health and welfare necessitating more and better site facilities, such as canteens, drying rooms, lockers and toilets.

When the preliminaries, priced by the contractors competing for a particular contract, are scrutinized, however, it is often observed that there is a wide variation in the prices. Expressed as a percentage for comparison purposes only, the preliminaries might vary between say five and twenty per cent of the contract price. This might be because the costs in the case of the lowest percentage have been allocated elsewhere in the bills. The lower percentage, however, often reflects cost cutting to obtain work and/or an inadequate assessment of the complexity of the work and the necessary project overheads.

11.3 EXAMPLE OF PRICING PROJECT OVERHEADS AND PRELIMINARIES FOR A THREE-STOREY OFFICE BLOCK (ESTIMATE 86/30)

The approximate value and the contract description form part of the process of building up a picture of the contract for management, thus helping them to envisage the consequences of obtaining this work.

11.3.1 Description

The building is of reinforced concrete construction with external brick facings, block internal walls and partitions, aluminium windows with double glazing, and a high standard of services and internal finishings.

Overall dimensions: 40 m × 15 m × 10 m high.
Area: The internal floor area is 1700 m².

		(£)
Approximate estimate: Building 1700 m² @ 460.00*		782 000.00
	External works including drainage	40 000.00
		£ 822 000.00

The rate per square metre (*above) may be obtained from an analysis of past tenders by the estimator or from published elemental cost analysis. This rate is, of course, only approximate, and will vary for different types of buildings and forms of construction.

It may be useful at this stage to refer back to the enquiring record and site visit report in Chapter 2.

11.3.2 Construction period

	(*weeks*)
Contract period (12 months)	52
less holidays	4
Construction period	48

The pre-tender construction programme should indicate the holiday periods, which nowadays may reduce the time available for construction by more than 8%; the time available may, of course, be further reduced by inclement weather, delays in the supply of materials or components, etc.

For convenience the programme from Chapter 2 (Fig. 2.4) is reproduced again (Fig. 11.1).

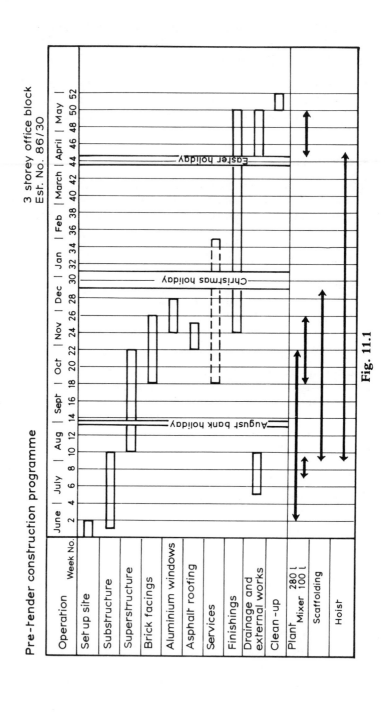

Fig. 11.1

Table 11.1 Programme schedule (estimate 86/30)

	Operation	Duration (weeks)	Week number
Set up site	See preliminaries	2	1–2
Substructure	Excavation and earthworks	3	2–4
	Concrete work	6	3–8
	Brickwork and blockwork to DPC	3	8–10
Superstructure	Concrete frame and floors	12	11–22
	Brick facings	8	19–26
	Aluminium windows and glazing	4	25–28
	Roofing	3	23–25
Services	Plumbing installation	10	
	Mechanical installation	14	19–35
	Electrical installation	6	
Finishings	Joinery (first fix)		
	Floor screeds		
	Plastering		
	Acoustic ceilings		
	Partitions		25–50
	Floor finishes		
	Joinery (second fix)		
	Wall tiling		
	Painting and decorating		
	Entrance doors		
Drainage and external works	Drainage		6–10
	Service connections: water/gas/electrical		
	Paths and paved areas	11	45–50
Cleanout and handover		2	51–52

This programme schedule has been prepared in conjunction with the pre-tender construction programme and shows the activities in more detail.

11.3.3 Labour force

When the main contractors work has been priced, the labour value can be abstracted and a reasonable assessment of the number of men on site calculated. These figures will enable a check on the supervision requirements to be made, and will assist in the assessment of the site accommodation and other relevant project overhead items.

Own labour value

Divide the own labour value of £99000 by average labour cost per week of £165 = 600 man weeks

Check this with the programme.

Since the programme times should be assessed on the quantities of work related to the methods and resources employed, the labour force will need to be calculated. Say the figures are as follows:

	Man weeks
Substructure, 7 men for 9 weeks	63
Superstructure, 12 men for 11 weeks	132
Brick facings, 6 men for 9 weeks	54
Finishings, 10 men for 24 weeks	240
Drainage and	
external works, 6 men for 11 weeks	66
Cleanout and	
handover, 4 men for 2 weeks	8
	563

The discrepancy between the programme assessment of 563 man weeks and the estimated figure of 600 man weeks is understandable and tolerable, since the estimate is calculated in much more detail and has taken account of minor items not considered in the programme calculations.

If there is a very large variation between the two figures, then both the estimate and the programme should be checked to ascertain why, and the necessary corrections can then be made either to the programme or the estimate.

11.3.4 Sub-contract labour force

The number of sub-contractors' men on site will also have to be considered in assessing the project overheads, since this will affect the welfare facilities to be provided. Similarly, the necessary overall supervision and co-ordination requirements must be considered as previously described in Chapter 9.

11.4 PROJECT OVERHEADS AND PRELIMINARIES— NOTES

As an aid to a methodical assessment, and to act as a check list, the estimator will usually use a pro-forma which is filled in according to circumstances. In the example there are nineteen sections, and no matter what size of job being tendered for, all of the items need to be checked to see if a cost will be incurred.

The following notes are intended to make clear how each section should be priced.

11.4.1 Notes on compiling the pro-forma

1. *Staff:* The staffing arrangements are a matter for construction management, and are invariably the most costly item of project overheads thus requiring the closest scrutiny. The programme will be found most helpful in assessing the type of specialist staff required and duration on site. It may be company policy to include direct supervision in the build up of the all-in-labour rates or gang costs. The rates, e.g. £260 per week for a site manager have to include for all direct on costs and thus can be regarded as an 'all-in' rate.

2. *Cleaning site:* A great amount of rubbish can accumulate on site unless cleared away regularly, this helps to keep the site tidy and safe. The use of rubbish skips and, on tall buildings rubbish chutes, is a great help.

3. *Site transport:* The transport of plant to and from the site is taken into account here as well as any transport, such as trucks or dumpers required on site that are not included in the unit rates.

4. *Mechanical plants:* In the examples given, the cost of fuel and lubricants has been taken as being included in the weekly hire rates. However, often this is not the case and an addition must be made to cover such costs.

   The cost of the operators has been taken into account in the calculation of the relevant unit rates.

5. *Scaffolding:* The cost of the scaffolding depends upon:

   (i) the type of scaffolding, e.g. independent, putlog or unit;
   (ii) the area required;
   (iii) the duration required.

   This work may be sub-contracted to a specialist scaffolding company who would require the above information in order to give a realistic quotation.

   In this case the method chosen is independent scaffolding obtained from an external hire company and erected by our own men. The overall time required is 20 weeks.

6. *Site accommodation:* The accommodation may be charged for either on a hire rate basis or on an 'on and off' charge.

   Rates are payable if the site accommodation is on site for more than 52 weeks.

7. *Small plant:* This represents the estimated expenditure on small items such as picks and shovels, wheel barrows, etc., with recent costs being related to labour expenditure.
8. *Temporary services:* Quotations should be obtained for specialist installations and any builder's work measured and priced in the usual way.
9. *Service charges:* The estimated cost for electricity may be calculated by considering previous similar contracts, and up dating for any increased charges. Telephone charges will be related to the location and the complexity of the contract as this will affect the distance calls have to be made and their number.

   Water charges by the Water Authority may be based upon the total value of the contract, or a meter installed (which has to be paid for), and a charge is then made based upon the actual amount of water used. In this case the value of the contract has been assessed provisionally at £822000 at a charge of £0.24 per £100 = £1972.80 rounded down to £1970.
10. *Welfare:* The cost of protective clothing will depend upon the number of operatives, the type of work carried out, and the weather conditions expected.
11. *Defects liability cost:* A suitable allowance should be made relating to previous similar contracts. It is usually considered that the probable cost is related to the labour and materials value.
12. *Hand over cleaning:* The preambles should be studied for specific requirements and it may be thought necessary to obtain a quotation from a specialist cleaning company.
13. *Transport men to site:* The National Working Rules have to be consulted to ascertain the necessary payments. In this instance it has been ascertained that the operatives will be travelling an average distance of 8 km, the relevant allowance being ascertained from the National Working Rules.
14. *Abnormal overtime:* When preparing the programme it was ascertained that the contract period would not be met unless extraordinary measures were taken. After due consideration, it was decided that the most economical method was to work overtime on the two critical operations of superstructure and brickwork. Two steps were then involved:
    (i) ascertain the number of man weeks when overtime would be required;
    (ii) ascertain the cost per man per week of the non-productive overtime.
15. *Security:* This may include the cost of a watchman, a private security service and/or floodlighting and security fencing. This can be very costly and will be affected by such factors as: the locality of the

contract, i.e. prone to vandalism; the period when the contract will be most vulnerable to damage or thievery, specific requirements in the preambles.

16. *Winter building:* The programme should be studied to see what work will be carried out during the winter; the trades of excavator, concretor, brickwork, drainage and external works being particularly affected by bad weather. Complex calculations may be required to ascertain the cost of: temporary shelters, insulation mats for concreting and brickwork, heating aggregates, etc.

    With reference to this project the programme indicates that the contract is due to start in June, and that most of the trades affected by winter will have completed their work by the end of November. Therefore, only a nominal amount has been allowed for the cost of protecting concreting and brickwork operations from rain.

17. *Clerk of works office:* Temporary accommodation and facilities are specified, if required, under SMM Clause B.8.1.j., and are priced in the same way as for the contractor's own requirements.

18. *Signboards and notices:* These are in part a form of advertising, but must be priced in line with anticipated expenditure. There may be specific requirements stated in the preliminaries, and the requirements of the Town and Country Planning Act relating to the maximum size of notice board may have to be considered.

19. *Sundry items:* These cover such items as testing materials specified in the preambles of the bills of quantities, and could amount to a substantial sum of money.

11.5 PROJECT OVERHEADS—ESTIMATED COST

See Table 11.2.

Table 11.2 Estimated cost of project overheads (estimate 86/30) (Contract period 52 weeks)

Item		Period (schedule weeks)	Number of weeks	Rate	(£)
1.	*Staff*				
	Site manager	1–52	52	260	13 520
	Foreman carpenter (formwork)	5–22	18	220	3 960
	Foreman bricklayer	19–26	8	220	1 760
	Finishings foreman	27–50	24	220	5 280
	Production controller 50% of time	1–52	52	160	4 160
	Site engineer 50% of time	1–22	22	200	2 200

Table 11.2 (*Contd.*)

Item	Period (schedule weeks)		Number of week	Rate	(£)
Chainman	50% of time	1–22	22	140	1 540
Storekeeper		24–50	27	150	4 050
Canteen attendant ⎱(part time)		3–52			
Cleaner ⎰			50	60	3 000
	Carried to summary				39 470
2. *Cleaning site*					
Labourer 8 hours per week			40	3.70	1 184
Rubbish skip : hire			40	5	200
loads	40			25	1 000
	Carried to summary				2 384
3. *Site transport*					
Transport: offices, scaffolding and mechanical plant to and from site	80 hours			10	800
Staff car (site manager)			52	55	2 860
Site van and driver 1 day/week			50	50	2 500
	Carried to summary				6 160
4. *Mechanical plant*					
Mixer 280 l (for concerete structure)⎱					
Silo 20 t ⎰			20	160	3 200
Mixer 100 l (for bricklayer)			30	27	810
Vibrators 2			20	22	880
Hoist, including safety gates			36	70	2 520
Pump and 40 m hose			6	40	240
Vibratory roller			4	25	100
					7 750
Installing and clearing plant	(£)				
Mixers	160				
Hoist	140				300
	Carried to summary				8 050

Table 11.2 (*Contd.*)

Item	Period (schedule weeks)		Number of weeks	Rate	(£)
5. *Scaffolding*					
External hire costs:	Total	1 140 m²			
First 4 weeks		380 m²	4	0.15	228
Next 4 weeks		760 m²	4	0.15	456
Final 12 weeks		1 140 m²	12	0.15	2 052
					2 736
Erect and dismantle	$\dfrac{1\,140\,m^2}{3\,m^2/hr}$	380 hrs		4.40	1 672
Internal hire costs:		210 m²	12	0.15	378
Erect and dismantle	$\dfrac{210\,m^2}{3\,m^2/hr}=$	70 hrs		4.40	308
Carried to summary					5 094
6. *Site accommodation*					
Office	30 m²		52	1.00	1 560
Stores	20 m²		32	0.70	448
Canteen	54 m²		48	0.80	2 074
Erect @ 1 hr	104 m²	135 MH		4.40	594
Dismantle @ 0.3 hr					
Base					
(foundations)	104 m²		2		208
Furniture and fittings: Staff		5		150	750
Operatives		20		30	600
Toilet block: 3 WC	@ 120	360			
4 Urinals	60	240			
4 Basins	80	320			920
Rates (payable if on site more than 52 weeks)					—
Carried to summary					7 154
7. *Small plant*					
1% of labour value £99 000					990
Carried to summary					990
8. *Temporary services*		(£)			
Electrics (lighting and power)					1 400
Telephone: Installation, including					
outside bell.		120			
Rental 4 quarters @ £40		160			280

Table 11.2 (*Contd.*)

Item			Period (schedule weeks)	Number of weeks	Rate	(£)
	Water:	Connection		140		
		Piping	50 m @ £4	200		
		Stand pipes	4 @ £25	100		
		Hoses and barrels		100		540
	Temporary access and reinstatement					300
	Drying out: Heaters and dehumidifiers					
		Hire		200		
		Fuel		300		500
		Carried to summary				3 020
9.	*Service charges*					
	Electricity			48	25	1 200
	Telephone			48	20	960
	Water (0.24 × £822 000 = £1 970)					—
	£100					
	see tender summary					
	Carried to summary					2 160
10.	*Welfare*		men			
	First aid materials (all operatives)		30		5	150
	Protective clothing (own operatives)		20		25	500
	Carried to summary					650
11.	*Defects liability cost*					
	1% Labour value £99 000					990
	½% Materials value £133 400					667
	Carried to summary					1 657
12.	*Handover cleaning*					
	3 Labourers			1	140	420
	Carried to summary					420
13.	*Transport men to site*					
	Including allowance for					
	labour in project overheads					
	(600 + 135) = 735 man weeks					
	@ average payment				1.70	1 250
	Average distance 8 km					

Table 11.2 (*Contd.*)

Item	Period (schedule weeks)		Number of weeks	Rate	(£)
Daily travel allowance	12p				
Daily fare allowance	22p				
	34p				
∴ 5 day week = £1.79					
Carried to summary					1 250
14. *Abnormal overtime*					
Superstructure	132	man weeks		15	1 980
Brickwork	54	man weeks		15	810
Carried to summary					£2 760
15. *Security*					
Hoardings: 108m @£12					1 296
Gates					100
Security service			30	50	1 500
Carried to summary					£2 896
16. *Winter building*					
Protection					500
Heating aggregates					400
Carried to summary					£900
17. *Clerk of works office*					
Office	15 m^2		52	1.00	780
Erection and dismantling	20 MH			4.40	88
Base	15 m^2			2.00	30
Furniture and fittings					150
Carried to summary					£1 048
18. *Signboards*					200
Notices					50
Carried to summary					£250
19. *Sundry items*					
Testing materials					400
Carried to summary					£400

11.6 SUMMARY

		(£)
1.	Staff	39 470
2.	Cleaning site	2 384
3.	Site transport	6 160
4.	Mechanical plant	8 050
5.	Scaffolding	5 094
6.	Site accommodation	7 154
7.	Small plant	990
8.	Temporary services	3 020
9.	Service charges	2 160
10.	Welfare	650
11.	Defects liability cost	1 657
12.	Handover cleaning	420
13.	Transport men to site	1 250
14.	Abnormal overtime	2 760
15.	Security	2 896
16.	Winter building	900
17.	Clerk of works office	1 048
18.	Signboards and notices	250
19.	Sundry items	400

Total carried to tender summary   86 713

SELF-ASSESSMENT QUESTIONS

1. Explain why a pre-tender construction programme is considered to be an essential aid to making an accurate assessment of the predicted cost of the project overheads.

2. How may the number of man weeks be calculated and to what use may this information be put at the tender stage.

3. If the start of the hypothetical contract is to be delayed until October, discuss the effect on the probable cost of the project overheads.

4. An alternative tender is required for a contract period of 48 weeks. Calculate the probable revised estimated cost of the project overheads. This will need every item of the project overheads to be investigated, and, amongst other things, an assessment made of the additional abnormal overtime requirements.

12

TENDER FINALIZATION

```
CHAPTER OBJECTIVES
```

After studying this chapter you should be able to:

- appreciate the overall financial background to a construction firm;

- analyse the resources employed in constructing a building;

- understand the process of converting an estimate into a tender.

12.1 PROFILE OF A MEDIUM-SIZED CONSTRUCTION FIRM

To follow the conversion of an estimate into a tender it will be helpful to consider some further background information concerning the 'typical' medium sized construction firm first mentioned in Chapter 2 under the heading of 'Management Services and Responsibilities'.

Some of the following information regarding the financial background of the company may be difficult to follow, but an estimator should have an overall view of a company's business affairs in order to work effectively as part of the management team.

Only selective aspects of the company's financial arrangements need to be considered in detail, for example the derivation of the general overheads percentage and the profit margin.

12.1.1 Breakdown of turnover into number and value of contracts

- *Number of Contracts.* Approximately fifteen contracts are in progress at any one time.
- *Type of Contracts.* General building work: factories, offices, shops, extension and alterations. It is all contract work, and is thus not speculative.
- *Turnover.* The turnover to year ended 31 December 1985 was £5 000 000.

Table 12.1 Work in Progress for Period 12 Months Prior to end of April 1986

Contract number	Value (£000's)	Contract period (months)	Start date
			1984
1	440	22	June
2	540	18	July
3	400	16	September
4	360	18	September
5	375	15	September
6	200	10	October
7	500	20	November
8	300	15	December
			1985
11	630	18	March
12	400	20	March
13	720	24	April
14	150	10	May
15	160	8	May
16	150	6	June
17	700	14	August
18	360	12	August
19	90	9	August
20	600	20	October
21	80	8	October
			1986
22	300	15	January
23	90	6	January
24	660	11	February
25	480	12	February
26	225	9	April

- *Contract Periods.* Contract periods usually vary between six months and two years. Contracts over twelve months being on a fluctuation basis.
- *Work in Progress.* See Table 12.1 for details of work in progress. The start date is assumed to be the first of the month. Value is taken as the contract sum.

12.1.2 Financial background

See Tables 12.2 and 12.3.

Table 12.2 Summarized Income Statement for the year ended 31 December 1985

		Value	
	---	---	---
Item	(£000's)	(£000's)	(£000's)
Value of work done			4978
Cost of work done			
Own work: Materials		840	
Plant Hire		114	
Labour		760	
		1714	
Subcontractor's work: Domestic	1800		
Nominated	414		
Statutory			
undertaking	31		
	2245	2245	
Project overheads		544	
General office overheads		310	
(including debenture interest)			
		4813	4813
Net profit, before appropriations			165
Corporation tax for the year		41	
Ordinary dividend for the year (12%)		90	
		131	131
Unappropriated profit for the year			34
Unappropriated profit, brought forward			176
Retained profits, carried forward			210

Table 12.3 Balance sheet as at 31 December 1985

	Value		
Item	(£000's)	(£000's)	(£000's)
Shareholders' funds			
Ordinary Shares:			
Authorised: 1 000 000 £1 shares			1000
Issued: 750 000 £1 shares, fully paid			750
Reserves:			
Share premium account		50	
Retained profit		210	
		260	260
Long-term liabilities			
8% debentures, secured on freehold property			90
			1100
Represented by:			
Fixed assets	*Cost*	*Depreciation*	
Freehold property (market value £400 000)	260	—	260
Plant and machinery	215	85	130
Motor vehicles, office equipment, etc.	95	35	60
	570	120	450
Current assets			
Stock of materials		140	
Work in progress (net of progress payments)		510	
Debtors		396	
Cash at bank and in hand		34	
		1080	
Less: Current liabilities			
Dividends	90		
Taxation	41		
Bank overdraft	57		
Creditors and accruals	242		
	430	430	
		650	650
			1100

12.2 GENERAL OVERHEADS

12.2.1 Definition

General overheads may be defined as the cost of administering a company. These costs are incurred off site, and may be explained by example (see detailed general overheads budget in Table 12.4). The accountant may think of general overheads in quite a different way, so that instructions must be given to the accountant to analyse the account in a form that will not only satisfy the auditors and the Inland Revenue, but give the requisite information to the company's management.

12.2.2 General overheads budget

A prediction of the probable expenditure in the forthcoming year is required so that these costs may be allocated in future tenders by the estimator. The expenses shown in the example may be obtained from an analysis of the accounts. This analysis must be checked regularly to ensure that the expenditure is controlled within the limits set.

It is usual to express the general overheads as a percentage of turnover less general overheads and profit, i.e. prime cost of work or total cost of direct labour employed by the main contractor.

12.2.3 Methods of recovery

There are several alternative methods of recovering general overheads each having particular advantages of simplicity of application or accuracy, but not usually both. Four examples are given here, but there are also further permutations:

1. Fixed percentage on the total estimated prime cost of the contract.
2. Fixed percentage on the total estimated direct labour cost of the contract.
3. Variable percentage, dependent on size and type of contract, applied to the total estimated cost of the contract.
4. Variable percentage, dependent on the size and type of contract, on total estimated direct labour cost of the contract.

Whatever method is used, overheads must be recovered in full, otherwise a loss will be made and the firm may become insolvent.

12.2.4 General overheads percentage

The percentage for the first described method of recovery will now be ascertained using the relevant figures from the 'financial background' of the company.

Prime cost (cost of work done excluding general overheads)

	(£)
Own work	1 714 000
Subcontractor's work	2 245 000
Project overheads	544 000
	£4 503 000

General overheads	£ 310 000
$\dfrac{\text{General overheads}}{\text{Prime cost}} \times 100 =$	?%

i.e. $\dfrac{£310\,000}{£4\,503\,000} \times 100 = \qquad 6.88\%$

If it is thought that either the prime cost expenditure or the general overheads expenditure will vary in the coming year, the figures should be adjusted accordingly, and the amended figures used in the calculation of the general overheads percentage.

The example of the general overheads budget given in Table 12.4 does give an anticipated increase over the expenditure last year.

12.2.5 Contract finance

The cost of financing contracts may be ascertained from a study of the company accounts and an average percentage applied to every contract, usually by including in the general overheads. Alternatively the cost may be calculated for each individual contract.

Cash flow

The contractor is usually paid monthly. This will therefore represent a cash inflow based on the value of work done less retention. If from the cash inflow is deducted the cash outflow represented by the payments for all the resources employed—materials, plant labour, subcontractors, etc.—the difference, which will invariably be negative until towards the end of the contract, will represent the finance to be provided by the contractor.

12.2.6 Finance costs to a client

The cost of financing a contract by a client is illustrated below for a contract carried out in either 10 months or 20 months and with loan charges at 2% per month.

Table 12.4 General overheads budget

Item		Section total (£)
1	*Personal emoluments*	
1.01	Directors and staff salaries	
1.02	National insurance, etc., for above	196 500
2	*Car expenses*	
2.01	Annual depreciation	
2.02	Licences	
2.03	Insurances	
2.04	Petrol and oil	
2.05	Maintenance	31 400
3	*Business premises*	
3.01	Rent, rates	
3.02	Gas, electricity (heating and lighting)	
3.03	Repairs and decorations	
3.04	Cleaning	
3.05	Fire insurance	33 800
4	*Indirect expenses*	
4.01	Apprentices time (day release, etc.)	
4.02	CITB levy on office staff (net after recoveries)	14 200
5	*Miscellaneous*	
5.01	Printing and stationery	
5.02	Postage	
5.03	Telephone	
5.04	Advertising including signboards	
5.05	Bank charges	
5.06	Loan interest	
5.07	Bad debts	
5.08	Insurances (burglary, etc.)	
5.09	Subscriptions to association etc.	
5.10	Depreciation of office equipment and furniture	
5.11	Company pension scheme contributions	
5.12	Legal and audit charges	42 100
	Estimated general overheads for the year	£318 000

This budget has been derived from the company accounts, and has been adjusted to allow for likely increase in the year ahead.

Case 1   Contract period 10 months and value £ 100 000

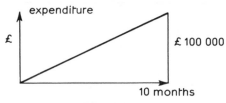

Fig. 12.1

Ref. fig. 12.1   Finance costs $\dfrac{£\,100000 \times 10\ \text{months}}{2}$ @ 2% = £10 000

Case 2   Contract period 20 months and value £ 100 000

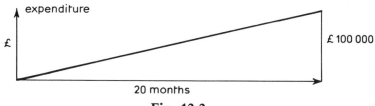

Fig. 12.2

Ref. fig. 12.2   Finance costs $\dfrac{£\,100000 \times 20\ \text{months}}{2}$ @ 2% = £20 000

The actual expenditure will usually be in the form of an 'S' curve, having a slow build-up initially and most of the expenditure occurring in the middle third of the contract period. However, the end result will be similar. Thus, it can be seen that the longer the contract takes to build the greater the finance charges. In the second case, not only would it cost a factory owner twice as much for these charges before revenue would be earned from production, but ten months production could also be lost.

12.2.7 Risk

Certainty seldom exists, and therefore there is a probability that the actual cost of any contract will vary from the estimate by a positive percentage.

This risk to the contractor is mainly confined to the value of the work priced by the estimator. In the case in question, the estimated cost of the main contractor's work is £327 777, or some 40% of the total contract value. Thus an allowance of 1% applied to the total nett cost of £726 747 in the tender summary amounts to £7 267 or expressed as a percentage of the main contractor's work only:

$$\frac{7267 \times 100}{327\,777} \times 100 = 2.2\%$$

12.2.8 Profit

The profit shown in the summarized income statement is nett, i.e. the total sum of money remaining from income after paying for the cost of work done including general overheads and amounts to £165 000. This figure may be expressed as a percentage of the cost of work done:

$$\frac{£165\,000}{£4\,813\,000} \times 100 = 3.43\%$$

If the figure were expressed as a percentage of the cost of work done, excluding general overheads, this would amount to

$$\frac{£165\,000}{£4\,503\,000} \times 100 = 3.66\%$$

The derivation and application of these percentages should be carried out in the same manner.

12.2.9 Tender margin

The tender margin is the difference between the estimated nett cost excluding general overheads and the tender figure.

In the tender summary the following assessment has been made:

	(%)
Risk	1.00—related to this contract
General overheads	6.88—related to the accounts
Profit	3.66—related to competition, the accounts, and past success rates.
	11.54 say 11.50%

12.3 TENDER SUMMARY

Finally, the estimator collates the figures representing the value of all the resources to be employed on the contract in a tender summary. This involves abstracting the materials, plant and labour values for the main contractor's work, and classifying the subcontract work under headings, giving the cash discounts, as shown in the following pages.

Prior to, and during, the above collation, a thorough arithmetical and technical check should be made.

The priced bills of quantities should also be checked for such errors as items being priced at incorrect unit rates, e.g. cubic metres instead of square metres, and incorrect interpretation of the unit description, e.g. a lineal brick coping being taken as half a brick thick, when it should be one brick thick.

Main Contractor's Work

The total estimated cost of materials, equipment and labour are abstracted from the measured works section and entered on the summary. The project overheads consist of a combination of resources, and may be analysed to give a detailed breakdown in a similar fashion to the rest of the tender summary.

Own or Domestic Sub-contractor's Work

It is usually a straightforward task to abstract these costs from the measured works section, except in the case of elemental bills, in which case it may be a case of separate items being abstracted. The priced bill submitted by the sub-contractor should act as a check.

Nominated Sub-contractor's and Supplier's Work

These figures are usually contained in the prime cost section of the bills. Care must be taken to abstract the relevant figures, any attendance being allocated in the totals of main contractor's work with profit being excluded (Table 12.5).

Table 12.5 Main Contractor's Work

Bill number	Trade	Material	Plant	Labour	Total
2	Excavation and earthwork	2 047.10	5 188.65	3 031.80	10 267.55
3	Concrete work	80 110.00	1 200.00	37 811.12	119 121.12
4	Brickwork and blockwork	26 700.00	—	31 126.00	57 826.00
6	Wood work	10 666.00	—	9 377.48	20 043.48
7	Metal balustrading (fix only)	—	—	280.00	280.00
13	Drainage	3 503.07	660.00	3 489.10	7 652.17
14	External works	12 159.10	2 510.00	13 990.46	28 659.56
	To tender summary	135 185.27	9 558.65	99 105.96	243 849.88

Cash Discounts

Any cash discounts on materials and plant quotations may be taken into account when pricing the unit rates or, with more difficulty, calculated separately and entered on the summary. Sub-contractors' quotations have to be analysed to calculate any discounts given. Nominated sub-contractors' and suppliers' discounts are dependent on the form of contract, and can readily be calculated and entered.

On the assumption that all payments are made within the time limits to qualify for a cash discount, the total of cash discounts receivable may be deducted from the sub-total to give a nett figure.

The figures below in Tables 12.6 and 12.7 have been taken from the bills of quantities and do not include for attendance or contractor's overheads and profit.

Table 12.6 Domestic Sub-contractors

Bill number	Trade	(£)	Cash discounts (%)	(£)
5	Roofing	9210.19	2½	230.25
8	Plastering and floor screeds	17172.26	—	
9	Granolithic and terrazzo floor finishes	2349.44	—	
10	Flexible vinyl floor finishes	18467.31	2½	461.68
11	Ceramic wall tiling	2119.67	—	
12	Painting and decorating	12323.94	2½	308.10
	Carried to tender summary	61542.81		£ 1000.03

Table 12.7 Nominated Sub-contractors

Item	(£)
Structural steelwork	1 500
Metal windows and entrance doors	37 000
Plumbing and mechanical engineering installations	140 000
Electrical installations	62 000
Lift installation	38 000
Glazing	16 500
Carried to tender summary	295 000

Table 12.8 Nominated suppliers

Item	(£)
Metal balustrading	800
Ironmongery	1 100
Carried to tender summary	1 900

12.3.1 Provisional sums

Provisional sums are deemed to include overheads and profit and should therefore be adjusted to a nett figure on the tender summary, since the profit margin is (in the example given) added at the end.

12.3.2 Bonds and project insurances

Bonds

A performance bond may be required by the client as a guarantee that the contract will be completed in the event of the insolvency of the contractor. These performance bonds are often called contract guarantee bonds and are sometimes required by local authorities and other public bodies—it is unusual for private clients to require such bonds.

Performance bonds may be issued by banks or insurance companies with the premium being related to the financial soundness of the construction company. If a bond is required, it would be prudent to discuss the matter with an insurance broker to ascertain if a bond would be available and what would be the cost.

Insurance

Insurance of the works against fire, etc., is usually required under the terms of the contract for complete buildings, but, in the case of alterations or additions, it is usual for the client to extend his existing insurance cover.

It is now becoming usual for the contractors to take out a policy generally for the risk of damage to the works they undertake, not for each particular contract. In this case the employer's interest must be endorsed on the policy (contractor's all risks policy). In this type of policy, cover against theft and vandalism is usually included.

Thus, the cost allocation to a particular contract would be calculated as follows:

Contract value £800 000 @ £0.14 per £100 = £1120.

12.3.3 Firm price addition

The contract is to be let on a firm price basis (clause 38-limited fluctuations) which is usual for contracts of one year duration or less. Where the contract period is for more than one year then the fluctuations clause (clause 40—price adjustment formula) would normally apply.

In this case suppliers of materials and subcontractors would also be asked to quote on a firm price. In the event, it is unlikely that they would be willing to accept this risk so the main contractor has to make as good an estimate as possible of the likely increased costs. The cost elements will now be considered in turn.

Materials
The estimated nett cost of materials at 20 May 1986 and purchased over the next 12 months is £133 471. The rate of inflation on materials has to be predicted over this period, and this should take into account price trends and, wherever possible, known statements of suppliers regarding their policy on say keeping prices stable in the near future.

In this case an increase of 7% per annum has been assumed and since materials will be purchased gradually over this period this will give an average increase therefore of 3½% on £133 471 =

(£)

4 671

Plant
The estimated nett cost of plant is £9 559 @ say 3% (excluding that plant included in the project overheads)

287
—

Labour
The estimated nett cost of labour at 20 May 1986 is £99 106. Wage rates are usually agreed every year, with the new rates starting from the end of June. Other wage related costs such as National Insurance and the CITB levy may be altered at other times, but the biggest influence is of course the annual wage increase—sometime we may achieve stability. An average increase of 7½% has been assumed and this will apply to 11/12 of the wages bill since only one months work will be carried out before the increase. £99 106 × 11/12 × 7½%

6 813

Project overheads and preliminaries
The estimated nett cost is £86 713, say average increase over 12 months is 3%

2 601

14 372

Own increases
Domestic subcontractor: nett value £60 543 at average increase of 3%

1 816

Total estimated allowance for firm price

£16 188

12.3.4 Value added tax (VAT)

Reference should be made to Notice no. 708 VAT regarding the application of value added tax to the construction industry, and notice no. 715 which deals in more detail with the application of VAT to alterations, repairs and maintenance.

Clause 15 (value added tax—supplemental provisions) of JCT form of contract 1980 should also be referred to. This states that the contract sum shall be exclusive of any tax. Any VAT properly chargeable to the contractor shall be reimbursed by the employer.

Generally speaking, new construction work is zero-rated. This applies to new construction or demolition of a building or civil engineering work.

Alteration, repair and maintenance work is always liable at the standard rate of tax, and includes such work as:

- extensions;
- interior and exterior redecorating;
- repointing of brickwork;
- re-roofing or replacement of slates or tiles;
- replacing gutters and rainwater pipes;
- renewing electric wiring systems.

All material invoices from supplies will have an addition for VAT and will be paid by the contractor. However, if the work is zero-rated this tax will be refunded by Customs and Excise. Where VAT is chargeable by subcontractors, utility companies and for professional services and the like then the same process will follow and VAT will be refunded if the work is zero-rated.

Thus, the estimator should not include for the effect of VAT in the calculation of unit rates or any other predicted costs to be included in the tender where the JCT form of contract is used. Where however this form of contract is not used then tenders for works of alteration, extension or repair and maintenance should include for the effect of VAT.

12.3.5 Adjudication meeting

A meeting is held prior to the tender submission at which, as indicated in Chapter 2, all the personnel involved in the preparation of the estimate may be present. This meeting reviews the preparation of the estimate and the probable resource and financial commitment of the company, with particular emphasis on potential problems and their proposed solutions. Following this discussion, and having regard to the commercial aspects, the directors will determine the tender margin, and consequently, the tender figure as shown in the tender summary.

TENDER SUMMARY

Table 12.8 represents our hypothetical tender summary.

Table 12.8 Hypothetical tender summary

	(£)	(£)	Cash discounts (£)
Main contractor's work			
Materials	135 185		1 714
Plant	9 559		—
Labour	99 106		—
	243 850		
Project overheads and preliminaries	86 713		
	330 563		
Adjustments: deduct	2 786	327 777	
Domestic subcontractors	61 543	61 543	1 000
Prime cost and provisional sums			
Nominated subcontractors 2½%	295 000		7 375
Nominated suppliers 5%	1 900		95
Provisional sums nett $\frac{100}{1115} \times £35\,000$	31 390	328 290	—
		717 610	10 184
Cash discounts—deduct		10 184	
		707 426	
Bonds and project insurances	1 163		
Water charges	1 970		
Firm price addition	16 188	19 321	
Estimated net cost		726 747	
Overheads ⎱			
Profit ⎰ 11.50%		83 576	
Risk ⎰			
Total		810 323	
Tender sum		£810 323	

12.3.6 Tender submission

The tender sum is now entered on the tender form as shown in Fig. 12.3.

```
Tender              Hypothetical contract

To:   Complex PLC



Sir

I/We do hereby offer to execute and complete the whole of the above Works in
accordance with the drawings, bills of quantities and conditions of contract
for the sum of:-
.....Eight hundred and ten thousand, three hundred and.......
.....twenty-three pounds.........................(£.810.323- 00 ).
                                                    and to complete
the whole within ......52.........weeks from the date of possession.

I/We agree that should obvious errors in pricing or errors in arithmetic be
discovered in the priced bills of quantities submitted by me/us before
acceptance of this offer, these errors will be corrected in accordance with
Alternative 2 contained in Section 6 of the 'Code of Procedure for Single
Stage Selective Tendering 1977'


This tender remains open for consideration for ........2.......weeks from
the date fixed for the lodgement of tenders.

            Dated this ....21st......day of ...May....19 86 .
            Name ........Building Estimating..............
            Address ......Low Easby.......................
                    ......Olicana.........................
                    ...................................
            Signature ...J. Bentley......................


The Employers do not bind themselves to accept the lowest or any tender.


The completed form of tender is to be sealed in the envelope provided and
lodged not later than midday on   21 May  1986   and will not be
considered if lodged after this time.
```

Fig. 12.3

12.3.7 Submission of the priced bills of quantities

The lowest tenderer will be requested to submit his priced bills of quantities for checking, as previously described in Chapter 1. Patently, the total of the BOQ summary should equal the tender sum—and this is not as simple as it may seem, since the tender margin has to be allocated within the BOQ. It is here that computers are invaluable, since the difference between the original nett priced bill and the tender sum can be accommodated by altering all, or any, of the unit rates by the necessary percentages rapidly and accurately.

12.3.8 Tender reconciliation

Unsuccessful tenders

Where tenders have been submitted under the Code of Selective Tendering Procedure, Contractors are notified of all the tender figures. In this event, a record can be made so that the figures may be compared and used to assist in developing the company's tendering and marketing policy. Where selective tendering has not been employed then the results are often circulated by the consultants, or, on occasion, may be obtained direct from the other contractors.

Successful tenders

The same initial recording will take place, but, in addition, a final reconciliation should be made by the contractor's quantity surveyors with the actual costs. This is a complicated task, because of the advent of variations and the effect of inflation and other cost factors. Further, the final results will obviously not be available until after the end of the contract, which may be in a year or more, being of little use in assessing the financial viability of tenders that are being submitted prior to this. This problem can be overcome to a certain extent if the contractor's quantity surveyors and accounts staff have developed a methodical system of periodic, say three monthly, reporting instead of leaving the reconciliations to the end of each contract.

12.4 COMPUTER-AIDED ESTIMATING SYSTEMS (CAE)

12.4.1 Introduction

Large contractors over the last twenty years or so have developed in-house computer-aided estimating systems using main frame computers. The computer is often used in a general way by the company, with the first application being accounting and pay-roll, using a standard program. Estimating software has been prepared by programmers in association with the estimating department. As writing the program and installing the software can cost several hundred thousand pounds, it is impracticable for smaller firms to develop their own systems and consequently commercial firms have developed general-purpose software for sale on the open market. Some of the large contractors are also now selling their systems to other companies, including providing the necessary training.

The Construction Industry Computing Association has reported that by January 1986 there were about ninety estimating systems commercially available. However, it has been pointed out that most of these systems are anything but easy to use, since they are of the first generation and there has been little time for feed-back from users. Further, the coding and operating systems used are not compatible with each other.

12.4.2 Micro-computers

Software systems are now available for micro-computers such as the Apricot XEN and IBM PC-AT as they have the capacity to operate the program, store the bill of quantities under consideration and process the calculations. These very powerful desk-top machines enable the processing (calculations) to be carried out as the estimator inputs commands and information via a keyboard, the results appearing on a visual display unit (VDU). The results are saved on a storage disk and printed output (hard copy) may be obtained at once or at some future time if more convenient. Thus the estimator is using his computer like a calculator and notebook and feels that he has the machine under control, able to perform a variety of tasks at amazing speeds.

12.4.3 Prime objectives

The prime objectives of a computer-aided estimating system for a large company may be summarized as follows:

- Price BOQ on basis of up-to-date resource costs and printout. This applies to the work of the main contractor in the measured section of the bill.
- Separate those items that have a total cost of £x and over. Based upon the premise that 10% of the items bear 90% of the value, this will enable the estimator to make the most effective use of that most scarce of resources, time, by enabling him to concentrate on the most important work items.
- Facilities for the estimator to vary the resource costs of all items; normally the items considered will be the 10% most important items.
- To present a Resource Summary Report.
- To present reports on the cost and/or time effect of using alternative methods or materials, sometimes in computing called 'what if' systems.

Companies will, however, have varying requirements depending on: the type and size of contract carried out; the degree of sophistication required; and the time and money available to install a system. Thus the smaller firm may well opt for a compromise that will satisfy the following:

- Provide a flexible database of bills of quantities items that can be amended as required.
- Hold a database of resources—material, plant, labour—incorporating costs, material quantities and outputs.
- Price the bill of quantities' items on the basis of the database, i.e. carry out unit rate calculations.
- Enable the resources or output standards to be amended to suit particular circumstances causing variations in costs, outputs or material quantities.

In essence, such a system follows the analytical method of estimating in common use and takes advantage of the computer's ability to calculate accurately and speedily. The unit rates are then written in the bills of quantities and extended in the usual manner.

The competitive market means that only between one in five and one in ten tenders may be successful, so that a fully comprehensive analysis of the bills of quantities may not be justified in terms of time and cost involved. Once a contract has been obtained though, the advantages to management of the planning and control information may well justify further computer analysis.

12.5 RESOURCE SUMMARY REPORT

The example given is derived from the hypothetical project.

Trade:	Excavation or earthwork	(£)
Code		
M	Material	2047.10
P	Plant	5188.65
L	Labour	3031.80
	Total	10 267.55
	Over-riding percentage 11.31	1161.26
	Grand total	11 428.81

The figure of £10 267.55 represents the nett figure in the bill. The over-riding percentage may be added to all the unit rates for overheads and profit, including adjustments due to late quotations and changes in costs.

A further detailed analysis may be made by the computer of adequate capacity using a suitable programme as in the following example.

Detailed resource summary
Contract: Hypothetical   21 May, 1986
Trade: Excavation and earthwork

Resource code	*Unit*	*Quantity*	*Rate*	*Estimate* (£)	
M Materials					
M 110 Hardcore	t	259.0	6.00	1554.00	
M 130 Granular fill	t	32.0	4.60	147.20	
M 140 Blinding	t	12.0	5.10	61.20	
M 300 Timber (earthwork support)	m³	1.5	189.80	284.70	2 047.10
P Plant					
P 010 Hydraulic excavator H 580	Hrs	102.0	13.60	1387.20	
P 015 Wheeled excavator JCB3C	Hrs	96.0	11.00	1056.00	
P 021 Tipping truck 6 m³	Hrs	220.0	9.80	2156.00	
P 120 Vibration roller 400 kg	Wks	4.0	25.00	100.00	
P 130 Compressor 250 CFM and tools	Wks	3.0	120.00	360.00	
P 205 Trench struts	Wks	863.0	0.15	129.45	5 188.65
L Labour					
L 001 General labour	Hrs	482.0	3.90	1879.80	
L 002 Banksman	Hrs	198.0	4.00	792.00	
L 012 Timberman	Hrs	90.0	4.00	360.00	3 031.80
					10 267.55

The analysis can be used for many purposes, for example:

- *Preliminaries.* An accurate compilation of the number and trade classification of the labour content is given so that site facilities and supervision can be more accurately calculated, rather than by the usual method of taking the total labour value and dividing by an average rate to arrive at the number of men. Further, the handling, storage and transport of materials on site can be considered in a co-ordinated fashion.
- *Planning.* The plant and labour analysis can be entered using a critical path or bar chart programme either manually or by using a computer program. Preferably, the estimating analysis should be compared with an analysis prepared independently by a planner so as to give a

check on the accuracy of both the estimate and the program. Any differences in labour or plant content should be investigated for possible errors and corrections made as appropriate, hopefully making the estimate either more competitive or saving the company from a probable loss. The loss on one contract may nullify profits on several others—better not to win a contract than be 'successful' on a loss-incurring contract.

- *Adjudication meetings.* 'What if?' questions can be discussed with immediate feed-back from the computer for example, if the works are to be completed in sections (sectional completion), can the construction sequence be amended, perhaps using additional resources to allow for earlier release of retention monies? If the overhead and profit margin is allocated to items of work that are to be completed early in the contract, what would be the effect on finance costs? Front end loading, as the last example is generally called, has the effect of enhancing the cash flow and may enable the contract to be almost self-financing despite the application of the retention clause.

12.5.1 Co-operation and compatibility

The capabilities of computers, the state of programming and market conditions have now combined to push computer companies towards standardization. International Business Machines (IBM), are the largest manufacturers in the world of computers and other manufacturers such as Apricot, now recognize the importance of making their machines compatible. Thus, software designed for IBM may be used for an increasing number of other computers without modification.

If quantity surveyors also used a compatible system, then it would seem logical that the contractor is provided with a disc BOQ in addition to the normal printed BOQ, thus eliminating a major chore for the estimator of having to code all the items.

12.5.2 Successful tenders

With successful tenders, computer analysis can be useful in the following additional work: material scheduling; detailed planning; cost and bonus applications; resource forecasting and cost control; monthly valuations of work in progress; fluctuation calculations using the NEDO formula. This makes the actual running of the contract easier, giving more effective utilization of resources and making staff more cost-conscious. The feed-back to the estimator regarding such matters as waste percentages, plant utilization and labour outputs can also be more accurate.

SELF-ASSESSMENT QUESTIONS
---

1. State the main elements contained in the general overheads of a building company and explain how the cost may be allocated in tenders.

2. List the items that would need to be checked in an estimate before submission to ensure that a contractor minimizes his financial risk due to human error.

3. Define the term 'Tender Margin' and explain how this may be calculated.

4. Prepare a tender summary for consideration at an adjudication meeting and explain why the management of a building company requires this particular form of analysis.

   The figures below have been derived from the nett priced bills prior to finalization of a tender.

	£
Own labour	116 135.00
Domestic sub-contractors	
Quotations offering 2½% discount	32 600.00
Nett quotations	62 217.00
Plant nett	8 211.00
Project overheads and preliminaries	99 653.00
Nominated sub-contractors	301 000.00
Provisional sums	40 000.00
Own materials	
Quotations offering 2½% discount	61 210.00
Nett quotations	71 121.00
Nominated suppliers	2 600.00

The following additional information is given:

Late quotations for materials have been received giving a nett reduction of £852.00

Insurance charges amount to £0.15 per £100.00 of contract value. Similarly, water charges are £0.24 per £100.00.

A firm price addition of £19970.00 has been calculated.

An initial allowance of 12% is to be made for the contract margin.

INDEX